A BOOK OF SECRETS

www.penguin.co.uk

A BOOK OF SECRETS

Finding Solace in a Stubborn World

DERREN BROWN

BANTAM PRESS

TRANSWORLD PUBLISHERS
Penguin Random House, One Embassy Gardens, 8 Viaduct Gardens, London SW11 7BW
www.penguin.co.uk

Transworld is part of the Penguin Random House group of companies
whose addresses can be found at global.penguinrandomhouse.com

Penguin
Random House
UK

First published in Great Britain in 2021 by Bantam Press
an imprint of Transworld Publishers

A CIP catalogue record for this book
is available from the British Library.

ISBNs 9781787633056 (hb)
9781787633063 (tpb)

Text design by Couper Street Type Co.
Typeset in 11.5/20pt Bell MT Pro by Jouve (UK), Milton Keynes
Printed and bound in Great Britain by Clays Ltd, Elcograf S.p.A.

The authorized representative in the EEA is Penguin Random House Ireland,
Morrison Chambers, 32 Nassau Street, Dublin D02 YH68.

Penguin Random House is committed to a sustainable
future for our business, our readers and our planet. This book
is made from Forest Stewardship Council® certified paper.

For Dad

CONTENTS

Let everything happen to you:

Beauty and terror.

Just keep going.

No feeling is final.

– Rainer Maria Rilke, The Book of Hours

I believe if there's any kind of God it wouldn't be in any of us, not you or me but just this little space in between. If there's any kind of magic in this world it must be in the attempt of understanding someone sharing something. I know, it's almost impossible to succeed, but who cares really? The answer must be in the attempt.

– Richard Linklater, Before Sunrise

How can I begin anything new with all of yesterday in me?

– Leonard Cohen, Beautiful Losers

KNOWING EVERYTHING

I was punched repeatedly in the head by Andy Hunt and James Ward when I was fifteen. They beat me up during a Duke of Edinburgh's Award trip to the Brecon hills, while I cowered in my Daffy Duck sleeping bag, trying to protect my face. I spent the next three decades despising them both. And then, recently, I heard that the adult Andy had suffered a brain haemorrhage, and after a lengthy ensuing depression, tried to kill himself by cycling into an oncoming truck. Andy had somehow failed in the attempt and instead only caused further damage to his brain. When I was told this story, thirty-three years of loathing dissolved instantaneously in my blood. Here was a bully, now bullied by fate, and a lingering childhood narrative had proved to be desperately and naively out of touch with merciless reality.

Between the ages of fifteen and forty-eight, the name 'Andy Hunt' had functioned for me as private rhyming slang. He and his cohort had sniffed out the jasmine-tanged redolence of the nascent poofter, and such was my capacity for shame in those days that I didn't entirely blame them for taking a swipe. But I had no doubt that they were *nasty*, and nothing since had served to assuage my conviction. However, Fortune had so greatly overstepped the mark in redressing the balance that the hatred I had been carrying with me felt grossly inordinate.

Aren't our worst moments generally characterized by behaviours that spring from a certainty in our judgements that turns out to be naive? The violent disgust and superiority felt by a powerful kid towards an effete one, and the weaker boy's ensuing thirty-three-year hatred of his tormentor, were both made monstrous by personal narratives that scorned any mitigating facts or nuance, such as how events might have later developed when we weren't looking. Conviction is all, and we suffer from an abundance of it when we need to feel strong. Not, note, when we *actually* feel strong. Those times are usually typified by a generosity of the soul. But when we must gather ourselves in the face of something mighty, or against whatever scares or repels us, we eagerly cling to whatever available fiction is most fortifying.

I have, for as long as I remember, been shy to voice such

certainty of judgement in company. Unless I'm with someone I fancy or am quickened by a second Old Fashioned, I am commonly paralysed by an awareness that I only know my small share of the story. Perhaps for this reason I've never beaten anyone up, but neither has it made me noble or humble. It is allied to the difficulties I sometimes experience when I find myself among others, especially those headstrong types who make no effort to meet one halfway. I note with disappointment my overeagerness to please, and a somewhat diffident, avoidant personality. Part considered Stoic and part mere spineless dodger of conflict, I am skilled at circumnavigating stress, but company often reduces me to something deferential, courteous and boring. So I see the traps in what follows through the next couple of chapters, which is my attempt to advocate a greater appreciation of nuance and ambiguity. Perhaps, as a popular teenage punchee, it is no more than a defence of a particular weakness to which I am constitutionally disposed. But perhaps all philosophies are.

I began writing this book in New York in 2019 and finished it back home nearly two years later, following a house move, a fiftieth birthday, the death of a loved one, and a global plague. Life, it turns out, can be difficult. But I presume that most of my experience of it is in essence unremarkable. Thus I hope that many of you feel the same types of unease, or will at least find some use for the thoughts I offer here. I'll draw on the lessons I have gleaned from my own ruminations, as well as the lunacy of those two years, and the great ideas of others to whom my work has led me. Partly with a view to making life a little easier, partly in an effort to worry less about difficulty. And to unearth new pathways to empathy.

The eagerness for certainty, then, is the starting point of our journey. Our destination, by contrast, is a little murky: a place between places that has never been adequately named. Some call it the Considered Life, but that strikes a note of lofty contemplation I'm not sure does it justice. 'Wisdom' is too grandiose, and I cannot offer myself as a guide to such a venerated terminus when this morning I spent ten minutes looking for AirPods that were in my ears. Perhaps, as with all great journeys, the travelling itself is the whole point, and the anticipated destination might be no more than a place to take your coat off and rest. So wherever you arrive, if along the way you've found an easier relationship with some of life's obstructions and new opportunities for compassion – towards both yourself and others, of course – then you know you're at the right place.

Certainty and taking offence

Excessive conviction is a trap our natures have set for all of us, and its scarlet distension is usually evident on both sides of any dispute. When I wrangle with my partner over who has more neglected the pile of Thursday's plates with their yellowed and bumpy terrain of stiffened Port Salut, and whether the more contemptible crime is omitting to load the dishwasher or forgetting to *un*load it, I engage in a join-the-dots exercise in selective storytelling. In *my* tale, my responsible nature emerges as self-evident, a kind of constitutional benevolence punctuated by forgivable, even endearing oversights. My partner's pattern, on the other hand, is one of persistent hypocrisy and neglect, and his rare moments of dependability are welcome but bafflingly incongruous.

I conjure this exaggerated contrast in our natures not because I actually believe it, but because my response to an accusation is to twitchily secure all doors and windows, blocking any access to the shame that comes with admission of fault. We argue because we are both affronted, each scrabbling to present the more compelling fiction. In anger or defensiveness, honest ambiguity is the enemy; we are fortified by the certainty that only comes with fiction. We concoct stories regarding the motivations of even those we are supposed to love the most — tales that may bear little relation to reality.

Increasingly we have seen that in terms of public offence, what matters now is not so much what was meant as what has been perceived; and when ill feeling is caused, how many mercurial voices can be roused in sympathy. The forces of mass near-anonymity afforded by our online world, where one can signal risk-free allegiance to one's in-group, have rendered public outrage almost effortless to foment. Hence expressions of indignation in a tweet have been shown to lead to far wider online contagion than anything pleasant: fake news and outrage spread six times faster than non-outrage, according to Tristan Harris, the president of the Center for Humane Technology, whom we will meet again later. Our online landscape so often resembles a pitch-black oily slope that draws us inevitably into a mire of discomposure. The greater the tension around an issue, the less of a place there is for nuance, which is the enemy of a good clear story.

Effect, then, has become more important than *intention* in matters of offence. Take a story outlined in Greg Lukianoff and Jonathan Haidt's 2018 book *The Coddling of the American*

Mind. The authors describe the case of Olivia, a student at Claremont McKenna College in California whose parents had emigrated from Mexico before she was born. Olivia wrote an article to the effect that she felt marginalized, and believed she had been admitted to the college only to fill a racial quota. She sent the essay to the academic staff, and Mary Spellman, the Dean of students, emailed her a response. The authors quote the Dean's reply in its entirety:

Olivia –

Thank you for writing and sharing this article with me. We have a lot to do as a college and community. Would you be willing to talk with me sometime about these issues? They are important to me and the staff, and we are working on how we can better serve students, especially those who don't fit our CMC mold.

I would love to talk with you more.

Best,

Dean Spellman

Olivia took exception to the word 'mold'. She took it to mean that the Dean was telling her she did not fit in. Olivia publicized her offence on Facebook: 'I just don't fit that won-derful CMC mold! Feel free to share.' The Dean later explained she employed the word empathically, because marginalized students had often used it when describing to her their own experiences. Still, furious demonstrations followed, and stu-dents demanded that Spellman resign. Two went on a hunger strike, and eventually the Dean was forced to step down. The effect – the *impact* – of that one word was what came to matter; her intention became irrelevant.

The Dean was hoisted on an essentially literary petard: the misuse of metaphor. The question of whether the use of 'mold' was an unwitting revelation of insidious, systemic racism throughout the echelons of the university, and/or was simply exposed to a cynical, least-charitable interpretation on Olivia's part, is an interesting one. It points to the ambiguous nature of a linguistic snare which now lurks in the marshy grasses of any public discourse. Politicians and TV personalities are daily humiliated for their use of an unfortunate comparison or turn of phrase. Excruciating similes can be particularly unforgiv-able, but metaphors are more subtle. As Laurence Scott describes in his beautiful book *Picnic Comma Lightning*, a good metaphor 'brings two things together according to a certain commonality, illuminating shared ground'. One aspect of a machine mould, stamping out repeated, indistinguishable figures on a conveyor belt, seems appropriate when we consider what we presume to be the worrying problem of under-representation among the CMC alumni. Other aspects are not highlighted in the same way: there is an *intentionality of design* implied by the image of a factory mould, which Dean Spellman is most likely not implying (the tenor of her email suggests a personal intention to preserve and increase diversity, although if we assume a deeper historical problem, this may be of little comfort). Thus one aspect of a mould is 'illuminated', and in its glow we note the weighting of the academic system. But 'on either side of the spotlit, shared ground . . . the metaphor preserves two darknesses'. The many aspects of a factory mould that do *not* resemble the university system are to be murkily excluded, as are, 'in the second darkness', those qualities of the academic soul-shaping which cannot helpfully be compared to an industrial die-cast template.

The inherent ambiguity of shaded areas and floodlit spots within these language games is important, because we are creatures who think by comparison. As I consider this, I am sitting in the appropriately dappled semi-light of a tree-lined spot in the grounds of Manhattan's Lincoln Center, now look-ing up from my MacBook screen to watch a sample of locals pass by. It is 2019, and New York is buzzy and busy. Directly in front of me, right on cue, and upon an ergonomic concrete rip-ple of a seat, alights a bird-like older lady of the New York City type: stick-thin, brutally stylish with severely chopped white hair, and supporting a pair of round, glossy glasses of such monumental diameter they threaten to topple her. In her hands she clutches two revealing objects: a programme of the Cen-ter's events for this season (led by a new production of *Porgy and Bess*) and an open Filofax overspread with wheeling ball-point handwriting, hinting at a still-rich life of friendships and engagements.

As I watch her darting, avian manner, I pigeonhole this pigeon of a woman. Something reductive in me scans snap-shots of similar souls I've retained from the Upper West Side, where I am living while I perform my Broadway show. I see them tanned and draped in summer white, accented with spat-tered patterns of chunky black and red bijouterie; standing in line at the pharmacy holding baskets of potions in cadaverous arms; crossing roads, diaphanous at a distance, before the shock of seeing the face-paint in close-up as they hobble by.

I skip over her humanity in a heartbeat and she is reduced to a conventional type, another example of the classification I hold in my mind for East Coast Biddies.

But now, again as if prompted, she stands up, having consulted her itinerary for the day, and I am startled by an inconsistency. As she moves in the direction of the box office, her feet are revealed to me for the first time and I see that she is not sporting the white sneakers *de rigueur* among her ancient tribe. My breezy expectations are crushed by the sight of a black, built-up orthopaedic boot. A shiver runs through me, prompted by the very *individual* experience of a broken foot so late in life. I imagine her falling in her kitchen: neat, glossy, I see my own parents' kitchen, but it is she who twists to the floor by the hob and suffers the audible snap of a metatarsal. All other old ladies vanish from my mind.

The sight of that boot flips me from a bright, gaudy cliché to a searing sense of her unlit uniqueness. Yet as I look at the other denizens meandering around the Lincoln Center's rectangular pond, I am still distracted by the obvious totems. A skinny teenager passes, wearing tracksuit trousers with white stripe and a reversed baseball cap. A young, gossamer Asian woman flourishes a similar cap, this time boyishly juxtaposed with a lacy cream dress of the nineteenth-century style, diagonally intersected by the pencil-thin strap of a tiny Louis Vuitton purse. Across the water, a large man is promenading with two fat bulldogs, and outdistancing him, a misplaced hipster strides, ankles to the wind. No matter how hard I try to see the individuality of these people, it shifts in and out of focus, overlaid by faint ghosts of others who have come before. I can fully hold on to neither the general nor the specific.

Like the way in which the idea of a factory mould (with its implications of intentional design) intersects with the problem of college diversity to form an illuminated area, these people seem to shift and overlap with their predecessors, like two spotlights finding and crossing each other in the night. My Unconscious Taxonomy of the Public at Large has its uses: it prepares me to approach people as appropriately as I can, to recognize signals of status or preference, to shift my presumptions, to not make a fool of myself. I must compare these people to the spectral forebears I have selected for them, in the same way that when I approach a new situation I am obliged to draw upon my experiences in previous, similar environments to find the best suggestion of how to act. We are seekers of resemblance, a fact that permits us to navigate our environment by utilizing shortcuts, avoiding things that look dangerous, recognizing what is frail, forming rapid assessments of people based on a few cues: in short, maintaining our particular model of the world. We must shift constantly between the particular and the universal, the present and past, in order to secure any chance of a comfortable future. *Where have I encountered this before? What does this remind me of? Who have I met like this?*

We consistently work by metaphor, via these overlapping, time-crunching, mutually illuminating comparisons of people, places, things. We live analogously to our own history. Thus the very fabric of the world meets us in a way that is fundamentally fluctuating, and to navigate it we must force its living contours into some recognizable shape. We reduce a vibrant complexity that envelops and includes us in its activities to a simplistic model of life that feels predictable but which has somehow cast us out from the role of participant to that of observer. Thus positioned, we forget we are caught up in the maelstrom, as malleable and unreasonable as the rest of them, and are ourselves, on occasion, a great source of pain.

Craft ales and political partisanship

Take the certainty of our political views. In his earlier book *The Righteous Mind*, Jonathan Haidt set out a compelling idea that differing moral 'tastebuds' correspond with how we identify politically. An increased sensitivity to threat, for example, has been identified as a classic right-wing typifier. If we are part of a group that has that sort of sensitivity, then we are likely to *sanctify* certain objects or ideas, to grant special status to symbols that might help marshal everyone against outside threat. Such figurative consecrations – such as that of one's national flag, the monarchy, or a particular religious idea – amount to ways of keeping the group strong. These charged images help everyone call upon a shared fiction when they need to conjure a Herculean, 'groupish' mindset in the face of the enemy. Such measures also help preserve the status quo. From such 'conservation' we of course draw the word 'Conservative'.

On the other hand, the Left's own particularly sensitive tastebud – and therefore a powerful trigger point when it comes to liberal rhetoric – is that of *compassion for the weak*. Traditionally among the Left there is little or no emphasis on symbols of authority and preserving the social order; in fact characteristically there is a progressive urge to overturn such things. Developing this distinction, Haidt demonstrates that our political leanings may well be traceable in large part to a genetic predisposition to seek out or avoid new experiences. This in-built personal proneness then acts like a 'first draft', before it meets a world which will encourage or frustrate it in a myriad of ways.

When I met Jon for lunch in a hotel near New York's Washington Square Park, I told him of an experiment I conducted with my team, drawn from his and colleagues' work, as part of the audition process for *Sacrifice*, a special of mine on Netflix. We plugged groups of righties and lefties into sensitive equipment that could read their autonomous systems − sweating, heart rate etc. − and then showed them a series of carefully selected, purposely provocative images. The data crunching confirmed that the Liberals were unconsciously triggered by images of the weak and helpless (kittens and the like) while the Conservatives fired up when shown images of threat (monsters, ghosts, etc.), precisely as Haidt and others have shown.

Then, in a second experiment to explore the delicacy of our political convictions, we wanted to see if we could change social-political views, at least temporarily, by priming right-wingers to feel *less* threat and lefties to feel *more*. Haidt's research had demonstrated that Liberals can be induced to think more conservatively when interviewed next to a smelly rubbish bin. The danger of contamination, he had shown, is another form of threat. Wariness of contamination sits deep in our evolutionary psyche, most likely from a time when eating poisonous food was a very present danger.

We set up our room with a puddle of fake vomit, a lingering stench of faeces, and detritus scattered throughout. As the left-wingers entered, we apologized for the environment, and explained there had been something of an accident with the previous group. We then asked them to take part in a visualization of what happens when the human body decomposes after death. All this was to encourage feelings of disgust. After this visceral priming, they were required to fill out a form which asked for their views on several hot topics. Sure enough (we could compare their answers to those they had given to very similar questions earlier in the day), the left-wingers now gave more traditionally right-wing responses. Inducing repulsion had been enough to cause a notable change. It's no coincidence that the metaphors of right-wing racist rhetoric have often summoned up images of filth and contamination, encouraging xenophobic group-think by stirring up a primeval feeling of threat.

Conversely, and in a separate session that day, the *right*-wing group were asked to imagine they had the superpower of invincibility. This was a recreation of an experiment by John Bargh, outlined in his book *Before You Know It: The Unconscious Reasons We Do What We Do*. The result of this preparation was to *reduce* feelings of threat, and sure enough the Conservatives' answers following this priming were demonstrably more liberal.

Experiments like these do seem to show the ambiguous, pliant nature of what we like to think of as unshakeable, rationally derived political certainties. We are very far from rational or certain when it comes to our political views. Jon describes the image of our rational mind as a rider sat atop an elephant, believing himself to be steering the lumbering beast (which signifies the emotional unconscious). In truth the elephant merely leans one way and the rider is pulled along. Our intellect then engages in a post-hoc rationalization of our actions, thinking it made a decision. Consider those times you've been asked to do something you don't want to do, and quickly found excuses as to why you can't, often fooling even yourself that they were genuine reasons. How readily, for example, the excuse of needing to protect an elderly parent during a convenient pandemic springs to mind when you don't want to spend time in someone's company.

Understanding the differences in these Left and Right moral urges is helpful when trying to convince the other side of a contentious issue. The climate crisis, typically seen as more pressing by those on the Left, is often communicated to all through images of desperate suffering, particularly the plight of those in badly affected countries. But this is a framing born of the Left's compassionate urge, and again and again it misses its mark, as the Right returns with what appears to be a baffling cynicism and indifference. The vital step, discussed by Haidt and only of late realized by policy makers, is to use language that will press the *groupish* threat-button of the conservative-minded. Headlines describing flooded coastal regions and decimated wildlife are unlikely to trigger action from the Right. 'Here is How Climate Change Threatens the American Way of Life' is more likely to hit the mark in the US.

In another experiment upon which our own was built (designed by sociologists Rob Willer and Matthew Feinberg from Stanford and Toronto universities respectively), a group of Conservatives were exposed to a message that encouraged people to protect the environment from 'desecration' and to safeguard 'the contaminated purity and value of nature'. This phrasing tickled at those moral sensitivities around contamination. Afterwards, compared to a group that had been shown language evoking the more familiar 'do no harm' principle, they reported more positive attitudes towards climate change legislation, and even a greater belief in global warming, even though the message hadn't mentioned any evidence or information along those lines.

I find myself drawn to examples of how threat affects our views because they demonstrate to me how our (and therefore my) seemingly considered convictions are in truth malleable and multi-faceted. Back in an economically fitful 2009, I had read that our buying habits lean towards the conservative when we feel less sure of ourselves. Unfamiliarity breeds discontent. Tropicana, I remembered, had been forced to revert to its longstanding image of a straw stuck into an orange after finding that a flirtation with a fearless new emblem (a daring glass of orange juice) had upset the breakfasting public seeking the familiar at a time of instability. 'When the brands that we use every day suddenly change in the middle of a recession, they're changing what is safe, what is comfortable for us,' writes Martin Lindstrom in *Buyology: Truth and Lies About What We Buy.*

Cutting forward to the first British lockdown of the 2020 pandemic, I was interested to see the pattern repeated. In the decade before COVID, the imbibing populace had grown plucky. Booze shops stocked up on obscure artisan ales, home-brewed lagers, and a million hipster gins distilled in the subway-tiled backrooms of gentlemen's grooming salons and local pop-up blacksmiths. Too hip for the customary hop, we now rolled our eyes at the familiar labels. Big Beer was under threat: in retaliation, the behemoths tried to look small, or started to buy up the artisan labels that were endangering them. The modest Cornish brewery Sharp's, known best for its dried-fruit-laden ale Doom Bar, was swallowed in 2011 for £20 million by Molson Coors, who count among their many other brands Carling, Cobra, Foster's, Grolsch, Peroni and Sol. The industry giants began setting up their own small brewer-ies with fresh and exciting labels, masquerading as craft but in fact craftily mass-produced. At the same time, some appealed to their traditional customers by sneering at the male artisan sipper with the derision of the boys' changing room: in a defensive expression of its own uncertain status, Budweiser's 2016 Super Bowl commercial bragged over a hammering beat that it was 'not soft' and 'not a fruit cup'.

Surveys since have delivered the unsurprising finding that craft beers are the favourite of the political Left, and macro beers the preferred beverage of the Right. And those suspect leftie sippers have been classified (by the investment bank Demeter Group) as 'explorers' with 'non-linear taste preferences' – an apt description of the liberal mind. Combined with 2017 research at the University of South Carolina which intimated that the shopping tastes of drinkers are *predisposed* when it comes to seeking out new experiences, these findings neatly resonate with Jon Haidt's notion of liberalism growing from a genetic predisposition towards embracing new adventures.

Digging deeper, I saw that in 2013 the *Washington Post* had reported on consumer data suggesting that 'Democrats prefer clear spirits, while Republicans like their brown liquor'. The difference in colour is due to tiny impurities, or *congeners*, which commonly come from the wood during barrel-ageing. They darken our malts and cognacs, augmenting the hangovers of the traditionalists. These drinks, with their marketing language of rich mahogany, age, tradition, maturity and patience, evoke all that is conservative: a nostalgia for a once great and now lost world, since surrendered to a bunch of fruitcups – the arch narrative of the Right.

After the confidence of exploration came the 2020 plague. Despite an initial spike in home-drinking, alcohol buying over-all dropped drastically as we confined ourselves at home: sales of beer tumbled around 80 per cent in the UK following the enforced closure of pubs, according to the Society of Independent Brewers. Most small breweries, reliant on social activity and events to attract attention, were forced to close. The thunderclap of threat sent us, like the Tropicana drinkers of the noughties, back into Safe Mode. Even the wine industry noted the shift towards conservative drinking: research agency *Wine Intelligence* anticipated 'a renewed focus on domestic and local wine in wine-producing countries, reflecting national populations becoming more inwardly-focused and protective'. Rarely has wine sounded as right-wing.

Threat has us crank up the drawbridge, revert to groupish patterns, and pull together under the canopy of broad and certain narratives. Whether it's beer or politics, we avoid the threat of the unfamiliar. We look for safety in numbers. A reluctance to experience the new might be in our DNA or merely a temporary response to the smell of sick, but what passes as a Left or Right political identity (and, we like to think, the stuff of rational consideration) turns out to be a touching expression of our ambiguous needs to sometimes change the world and sometimes hide away in it.

When we need to grasp the comforts of convention to our blimpish bosom, its totems (such as that Star-Spangled Banner) are deemed holy and thus off-limits to criticism. It's a fascinating mark of our times that this religious mode has crept around to the far Left with fresh vigour. On both edges of the political spectrum, like a Möbius strip that folds around on itself, the quasi-religious mindset of sanctification identified by Jon Haidt emerges when – majority or minority – we want to keep our group strong and protected from the enemy without. As lines are drawn on both sides, narratives are mistaken for gospel, the ambiguity of nuance is lost, and opportunities for understanding soon dispensed with. Increasingly on the Left, dissenters who raise nuanced questions that threaten the prevailing and loudest-preached narratives are commonly met with wild-eyed damnation, and face the eternal torment of social media stake-burning, or worse. We have been made aware of the Original Sin of inherited privilege, which damns us from birth like Adam's dark legacy, regardless of our circumstances. There is in the air a devout mindset, a drawing up of Good and Evil, aided by the proselytizing opportunities of social media that spread outrage faster than anything. Not surprisingly then, this stark polarization has its roots in the dark days of the old gods.

Good and Evil

In the sixth century before Christ, one of the oldest religions in the world, Zoroastrianism, made the bold move of dramatically reducing the varied pantheon of gods revered in Ancient Persia to a streamlined, cost-effective set of two. One god of this mystical binary deified the destructive, chaotic principle, while the other was bounteous and creative. The dualist theme was developed later in the third century AD by the Manichaean religion, which drew on a cosmic struggle between Good and Evil, now equating the former with the Spirit and the latter with all things worldly and corporeal. Mani, its founder, fused aspects of Zoroastrianism and Buddhism with an underpinning of early Gnostic Christianity (which favoured mystical knowledge over the traditional authority of the Church). According to its narrative, Darkness was a contaminating force that defeated Light, and seized control of certain of its aspects, creating the heavens, our world, and the first of us humans. We thus are congenitally contaminated by evil. Light meanwhile fights to regain dominion over these darkened areas. As human beings we are to understand that our souls are of divine origin, but they have become incarcerated in evil physical bodies. It is up to us to divorce ourselves from these ignoble frames and from the world, and seek a purely spiritual communion.

This religion proved very popular, penetrating the Roman Empire and becoming a strong rival to nascent Christianity. Awkwardly, Mani taught a 'corrected' form of Christianity, and preached that salvation from evil could be achieved through contemplation and a more profound knowledge of reality (*gnosis*). He made an enemy of the priesthoods of both Rome and Byzantium, who had no interest in sharing their prized and secret knowledge. Mani, the missionary, was tortured and flayed to death by the Persian ruler Bahram I. His body was cut into two, in a cleaving of morbid irony, and his severed head impaled on the gates of the Sassanid Empire's capital city, Gundeshapur.

The legacy of these paradigm-shifting religions, and the compelling narrative of Manichaeism in particular, has been to make it very easy for us to reduce conflict in the world to a fight between good and evil, right and wrong. America is frequently criticized for its Manichaean tendency to see its motives as self-evidently good, and any resistance from outside as bizarre, aggressive and presumed to be undergirded by methodical cunning. The language of goodies and baddies has threaded through US foreign policy rhetoric at least since the time of the Cold War. The theme of Good v. Evil was harnessed then to demonize the Soviets, again employed in Bush's invocation of an Axis of Evil and his attack on Terror, and more recently Trump's divisive tub-thumping stirred up domestic soil. At home, our own foundering relationship with Europe, shrilly evoked through the headlines of the *Daily Mail*, has seen much of the same. 'Enemies of the People' screamed my parents' copy of the paper when our judiciary deemed that a successful vote in Parliament would be necessary to trigger Brexit. In their defining mode of apoplectic outrage, one judge was damned as an 'openly gay ex-fencer'.

A Manichaean world view is identifiable when one sees one's cause as naturally Good, and anyone who questions it as Bad. Especially, that is, if the Bad group – which may be the outside threat, the dissenting voice of the press, or one's privileged oppressors within society – are unfailingly presumed to possess a consolidated agenda. The messy *ambiguity* of the true picture (and with it any opportunity for constructive dialogue) is sacrificed for the sake of a clear story.

In some situations – those of a national emergency, for example, or a tipping point of revolution – cohesive, unambiguous stories are vital. A reductive, single-minded vision may be necessary and any hint of indecisiveness could spell disaster. Thus in the UK we were rallied at the start of the coronavirus outbreak with the government's distinctively military language. Philosopher Nigel Warburton noted in the *Times Literary Supplement* that such language permits 'politicians to enforce wartime measures – "because this is after all a war" – none more extreme than those of Viktor Orbán in Hungary, who has given himself the power to rule by decree for a period with no specified end date'.

Remember the crisis-sickness we suffered before COVID? It was spread by too many passionate certainties. Brexit, Trump and the strains of identity politics left many convinced that we were in the midst of perpetual catastrophes from all sides, each demanding from us the strongest level of unambiguous, vocal conviction. Our group-urge, normally associated with the Right, was being tickled and brought to the fore. Propagandists have always liked to speak as if their situation has become critical, which justifies a reduction of language to the Manichaean. 'If we believe that our ideas must prevail to address a situation of social and political emergency, we will probably care little for whatever grains of truth can be found in the speech of our opponents,' writes Russell Blackford in his 2019 book *The Tyranny of Opinion*. 'Propaganda techniques can be used for exactly the purpose of bypassing rational deliberation about how catastrophic our situation has become. There's a temptation for controversialists – especially those on the political extremes – to depict each and every situation that they care strongly about as involving some enormous crisis, a state of emergency.'

The language of catastrophe justifies hostilities by activists; meanwhile, their action convinces us that we must indeed be locked in a critical state.

On this note, consider the recent reversal of antipathy

between old and young. Remember pre-COVID when the young railed at the rest of us for not taking climate change seriously? At the same time, the older generation was accused of bigotry of all sorts as any remaining respect for the Wisdom of Age was abrogated by the Moral High Ground of the Woke. The elderly, of course, are destined to lag behind every new cultural development: such is the natural antagonism of new and old systems. It is the patricidal, Oedipal foundation of progress, and at that point it was getting particularly vocal. But in 2020, us grown-ups, masked and wary, looked on in horror as a young generation partied in defiance of lockdown rules. I watched the east London streets I knew jam and choke with sangria-seeking hipsters; the parks were fuller than ever with frisbee-tossers and justice-warriors. For most of the lockdown the train from Brentwood to Liverpool Street still brought us its zombie armies of screaming hens and coked-up lads who regularly pissed or shat in our doorway; local bars and nightclubs remained at thumping full capacity; and throughout even the strictest times of quarantine, AirBnB was earning well from the flat next door to us which had become a crowded oasis for staycating euphorists and the narcotically compelled.

That *How dare you!* charge of criminal selfishness, once hurled with certainty by the young at a generation whose irresponsibility and baffling apathy threatened their future, may have now lost its edge. No doubt as the dust settles, old certainties will return.

HIDDEN AMBIGUITIES

I remember moments of my own excessive certainty: my many years as a Christian patiently explaining to anyone who would listen how Jesus *must* have risen from the dead. There was simply no other explanation for the events that took place – events, that is, described generations later in the somewhat partisan Bible, which on reflection may not be the most reliable historical source on the topic. To use a comparison offered by Richard Holloway in his gorgeous book *Stories We Tell Ourselves*, I was indulging in a religious form of mansplaining.

There is a difference between someone who has immediate experience of something, and someone who has learned about that same thing second hand. And although I would have insisted that I had a personal experience of God, I was of course taking my cue from the teachings of a religion – a set of ideas about which I'd read or been told. But I did not treat it as a philosophy I had merely come to understand as best I could.

Instead its very nature insisted I talk and think of it as *an entire transformation of my identity.*

I think of professional identities for myself: 'mentalist', which I know is true, and 'artist', which I'd quite like to be true but about which I am far less confident. I paint, certainly, and I sell the paintings, but to describe myself as *an artist* without pause requires a level of self-regard I have only seen in Americans. Now, were I required to justify my position as a professional mentalist, I would have no need for pretence or bravado. But if for some reason I had to convincingly defend myself as an artist, I would have to plug all sorts of gaps in my certainty with a broad brush and colourful confidence. I would think about how proper artists speak and behave, and reproduce what I could remember. My cues would have to come from outside of my own lived experience, in order to present what I thought should be seen. Such excessive conviction would be a sign of the fundamental, intolerable vulnerability of my belief.

Richard Holloway (he of the religious mansplaining) is the former Bishop of Edinburgh, and now a controversial figure in the Church. He describes himself as an 'after-religionist' and has written several excellent books exploring the value of doubt and ambiguity which he sees lacking in matters ecclesi-astical. He comments on how our need for certainty derives from the absence of direct knowledge which is an inevitable consequence of the passing of history:

> Whenever a spiritual revelation is enshrined in an institu-tion invented to carry its meaning through time, it is easy to understand how its guardians can become overprotective of the treasure they are responsible for, especially if their access to the original vision is theoretical rather than experiential . . . there is a clear tendency in subsequent gen-erations of believers to overdefine and concretise the original revelation.

They also, he continues, 'divinise or come close to divinising' the one to whom the original revelation came. He draws a comparison with political revelations: 'Marxist-Leninism, Maoism and Fascism all have the same characteristics as fanat-ical religious movements, the same tendency to deify their founders and dear leaders, and the same capacity for brutal authoritarianism.'

It will always be the job of organized religion to, well,

organize. A strong narrative to bind the group is the corner-stone of that task. And how eager we seem in life for such steadfast stories, and more than happy to leap over the cracks where we find them.

I find something touching in the way each of us faces the world as a lost child, looking for any information to show us who we are and what we should do, and how, despite our self-assurance to the contrary, we meet that information with more or less complete susceptibility. Conspiracy theorists may be dangerous figures within our information environ-ment in which shock and indignation spread fast, but I'm not sure there is a clear point when a person becomes one. In many ways and regarding many topics, we are each building separate, often incompatible worlds based on mistaken, faked and second-hand information, then defending them as if our identity depended on it.

This is the work of our nervous egos. If we wish to grow up or have any chance of seeing the world for what it is, and avoid-ing destructive over-certainty, we need to learn how to let *un*certainty and ambiguity sit.

Consider our natures, and the state of ambiguity into which we are born. We are living, but also dying. At some point we must reduce that fact to a more convenient narrative which allows us to make sense of our lives. The Existentialist movement of the twentieth century offered us another fundamental point of ambivalence: we are both the experiencing subjects of our own world, and objects experienced by others in theirs. We are free yet confined, proudly independent yet reliant on other people. The more we believe ourselves to be self-sufficient, the more we become aware of the degree to which our existence is tied to that of other people. What we are as an experiencing *inside* and what we are as a looked-upon *outside* seem locked in a constant tension. Yet to make sense of ourselves and navigate through the world, we must pretend we are one clear thing, and we must believe that we are always making plans and working to fulfil them, even though when we look back on our life we may note we have arrived in the present without real intention, dragging behind us a scattered history of first steps and false starts that rarely led anywhere.

We are also, famously, the conflation of reason and emotion. Aristotle, that great investigator of our flourishing, saw the good life as principally a matter of steering a course between the extremes of temperament: of embodying, for example,

courage rather than the too much/too little extremes of reck-
lessness or cowardice, or middling *confidence* in place of either
arrogance or timidity. To steer that virtuous path we need
strength of character, and to employ reason to temper our emotions. If we accept Aristotle's vision, we must note the
ambiguous tension inherent in every good quality that would
threaten to pull us towards its excess or deficit, as well as the
interplay of the rational and sensuous spheres. The Classical
approach to virtue is rooted in our equivocal natures.

We have largely forgotten the role of Fortune in our lives, of
which the Greeks were very keen to remind us. The very pride
against which they warned us is embedded in our modern
mantras of goal-setting and self-belief. The Ancients alerted
us to the fact that while we may try to fulfil our ambitions, we
do so at the mercy of Fate. Two thousand years later, in his 1851
Counsels and Maxims, the influential German philosopher
Arthur Schopenhauer would express it thus: 'Events and our
chief aims can be in most cases compared to two forces that
pull in different directions, their resultant diagonal being the
course of our life.' The single-mindedness we often adopt as
we try to control our fates will be our downfall; the Stoics and
Epicureans of the Classical era pointed us to the value of

moving in an easier accordance with Fortune rather than acting as if we can control it.

Schopenhauer also had us trapped between pain and boredom: we desire, we experience pain, we get what we want and are happy for a short while, we grow bored, we desire again. Without the pull of these twin poles, we would not move on with life: in short, we would not survive. Again, we note an equivocal, complex, active relationship with the stuff of life. Schopenhauer's 'diagonal' prefigured Sigmund Freud's vision, in which we are caught between wishing to express our animal, sexual instincts and the demands of a civilized society that deprives them of oxygen. In all these cases, our relationship to the outside world is caught in a persistent vacillation. Ambiguity is inescapable: it is the natural state of the world and our relationship with it.

Shadowlands

Here, then, are our slippery selves, with every face we show hiding its opposite. We're told even our kindness suggests sublimated aggression. We're a jumbled bag of humblebrags and contradictions; shorthands such as reason v. emotion seem merely to cover one eye and then the other like an ophthalmologist switching the lenses in a trial frame. The truer glass would be the child's kaleidoscope: tumbling colours returned in a multiplying geometry of mirrors.

Yet as we do in politics, so too we insist on artificially disuniting our inner selves. Witness how we learn to divide our own behaviour and impulses into 'right' and 'wrong', and then seek to banish the wrong. We emerge into a powerful, enormous world, populated by looming grown-ups who seem to know what they are doing and why, and who must have all the answers we need. One way or another we internalize a deep message that we are *not* powerful and that we are *small*. At first, our response is to scream, to alert the world when we are in need. Usually our caregivers rally around to give us what we want, any time, day or night. And thus we establish a kind of infantile entitlement, which we must slowly shed in order to become functioning social creatures. So gradually, good parents must let us down, disillusion us, teach us that we don't always get what we want. Some of us never learn, and remain screaming children into adulthood, baffled and furious when the world doesn't give us what we expect.

We continue to try things, say things, experiment, are encouraged or told *no*, and slowly we learn how to behave – what to show and what to hide. Sometimes, though, we bury parts of ourselves because they have proved unacceptable. Those unwanted parts of us have a habit of growing into charged, uncomfortable elements of a fuller self we are not honouring. Perhaps a child learns early that her temper is not to be expressed and responds by stifling *all* feelings, growing up oddly cold and unreachable. A boy showing 'girlish' traits is punished by an intolerant parent, and emerges as an adult who crusades against homosexuals, the effete and himself. Fledgling artistic experiments in another are shut down, along with all recognizably creative impulses which are barred by the psyche. But in each case, the person remains in the undead grip of what won't stay buried.

In this way, we inter our unwelcome parts, which may well retain a freehold over us, betraying the energy they have retained. Deleted from our ego's self-image, they are written out of our narrative, and we pretend they don't exist. But like those unfortunate characters in children's tales who are banished from the land by a fierce ruler (fairy stories so often resonate with us because they can offer useful templates of how our psyche works), they frequently return fortified by armies. While we choose to 'own' certain of our qualities, we also forget that it is precisely what lurks unseen that truly owns *us*.

Thus as we deny ambiguity in our natures, those parts of us with which we refuse to engage have a habit of wreaking revenge. From what the legendary psychoanalyst C. G. Jung called our Shadow side, they demand attention and reintegration. (It's worth mentioning that some of Jung's notions can seem a little fruity from today's perspective but the structure of his thought remains enormously valuable.)

Until they receive it, our unacknowledged aspects will nag at us, determined to be heard. The nagging may take the form of our patterns of addiction and avoidance, the emergence of things that obsess us, or the repeated occurrence of certain problems in our relationships. We attribute these issues to the unavoidable nature of other people or the inevitable drawbacks of our preferred sex: somehow, we hold the world responsible. We forget that throughout those recurrent disappointments, the only relentlessly present and true common denominator has been us. *Us*, indistinguishable from our peculiar, personal, galvanizing complex of preoccupations and over-sensitivities. Untended, undeveloped qualities, which we shut down early because we learned they were inappropriate, have set up king-dom in our badlands. And like those exiled, unwelcome gatecrashers of fairy christenings, they revert and lay their curse.

We have cultural Shadows too. Since the Enlightenment of the seventeenth and eighteenth centuries we have written ourselves into a powerful narrative of progress, of under-standing, and of the pioneering human intellect. And we have proudly redacted from the human story any value that might be found in myth, spirit, even superstition and the unques-tioned authority of religion. This turning away has brought an extraordinary age of accelerating technology and a richer understanding of our place in the cosmos. But when we bury these age-old aspects of ourselves, we lose track of our needs.

Myths, like fairy stories and the rich narratives of religion, are powerful by virtue of their psychological resonance. They seem to have developed in part to support the human experi-ence as we seek existential signposts to guide our way. For example, folklore surrounding death and what happens there-after may be *factually* untrue, but it can nonetheless remain *psychologically* legitimate. It has doubtless aided many in their final days to believe that the soul endures beyond bodily death.

Furthermore, an underlying notion of spiritual survival has surely encouraged us to remember the dead and therefore *learn from our pasts*. The religious myth of eternal life may not be just a balm to ease the pain of our last days, it may also have persisted as a means of preserving cultures by keeping the lessons of history alive. If our forebears watch over us in spirit form, we are more likely to esteem our past, and perhaps more deftly avoid the catastrophic pitfalls of the unchecked human spirit.

Likewise, despite my fellow atheists' easy scorn, it may be at some level useful to hear of a man who dies on a cross and returns in greater glory, because His story may function as an elevated re-telling of aspects of our mundane selves. It can be not-true and true. In life we must, in a thousand small ways, experience death and rebirth within. We are unlikely, for example, to find ourselves in a happy and lasting relationship without having dealt with the sad end of previous romances, and we cannot grow without letting go of some comfortable aspect of our former selves. Sometimes we must abandon the harmful patterns of an old life entirely. It is good to be told that we can rise again, transfigured when we do. Those great tales of gods returning empowered from the dead, shared across many religions and disseminated through innumerable death-and-return superhero movie plots, offer a value in their fortifying message for a species that must daily navigate and reflect upon adversity. Even as non-believers we might choose to respond less defensively to religion and acknowledge that beneath any horrors or silliness, it may still articulate (however badly) something worthwhile for us as we try to make sense of an unlikely and difficult existence.

The logic of myth once defined the ceremonies that supported us through the stages of life. Traditional rites of passage would have resonated with our developing psychologies and helped us find a sense of place and purpose. Consider: these rites often involved a child's separation from its parents and a dramatized death and rebirth of dependency; the communication of secret tribal myths and instructions for adult life to the wide-eyed adolescent; a staged ordeal through which they must develop inner strength; and finally the return to the fold, sometimes with a new name, ready to play a beneficial role in the community. Useful stuff. And such rites can still be observed among communities we like to think of as primitive.

Without a manual, we struggle to find our place in the world. Lacking a supportive, shared story of the developing soul, we flounder in adolescence and an empty stupor frequently settles in the pale-walled halls of dull and unheralded middle age. It is not that I am petitioning for a return to a more superstitious mode, but Myth, the banished, wicked godmother, unwelcome at the celebrations, may have laid a curse that now ensnares us in her grip. It plays out in a cultural norm of free-floating depression; panicked affairs and broken marriages; a mania for charlatans peddling cheap spirituality; a zillion flaccid self-help books; a lack of community feeling; the murderous radicalization of young souls searching for meaning; the estrangement of our elderly; the panic, absurdity and loneliness of the modern Western death.

The denial of ambiguity

It's difficult to maintain a comfortable relationship with uncertainty when we seem hardwired to cling to patterns. Our tendency to reduce a starry constellation to simple shapes (and likewise messy events to the sleek arc of a storyline) has created a strange rule in life that the more we truly understand something, the less certain we tend to be about it. The converse situation is familiar enough to us: people who don't fully understand a topic tend to have disproportionately confident answers about it. The less you know, the less you know what you don't know. This is the Dunning-Kruger effect, and it is more than evident in every reactionary tweet, every talent-show contestant's protestations at her summary disqualification, every toddler's temper tantrum.

Mature understanding, on the other hand, always brings with it an appreciation of complexity, and therefore introduces our friend ambiguity. True comprehension of an issue negates a child's story of right and wrong. This is the nature of growing up.

Meanwhile, the refutation of uncertainty leads to fundamentalism. A fundamentalist of any kind has locked the door on his own Shadow side and is pretending it has no validity, in himself or in others. And thus he is always on the defensive, always fearful. Without the capacity for dialogue within himself, he can only project his desperate need for certitude upon a world which can never provide it. Then when we add power to the mix, we create tyranny. If we refuse to see the world as complex and ambivalent, we will need to enforce inevitability in our environment and beyond. Irrespective of its source, this is the unlovely result of reducing the world to a battle of Good and Evil, of Them and Us, and the blind refusal of empathy.

The ambivalent future

We might also, here and there, more readily accept the ambiguity of what lies ahead for each of us. Life rarely goes according to plan. We know this because our lives so rarely have turned out as we intended, and things have never arrived in quite the way we thought they would. Yet we maintain the illusion that we are fashioning our destiny with every intention we proudly stake in the world: without this pretence, how else can we move forward?

Conviction is a story we tell, a state of mind. We know that the probability of a die rolling a certain number might be one in six, but it is surely an error to extend the same closed-circuit certainty out into the complex and contingent world of what, say, will happen following an event such as Brexit. Things will be what they will be, we'll seek to change what we can, and we will all use hindsight to draw up comfortable patterns of cause and effect to confirm what we are certain we always knew. The

confident lines we draw cut through a complexity or unknow-
ability which would otherwise prove too baffling to maintain.
Thus, our certainty is often just a symptom of how little intricacy we are willing to endure.

If this cosmic shrug feels a little too resigned in the face of
future happenstance, there is another resource that might help
us face the contingencies of the future. It comes unsurprisingly
not from Greco-Roman thought but from the Ancient Chinese.
The East has not seemed to inherit the Manichaean reduction,
and its tradition sees opposites not in tension but as comple-
mentary, even mutually dependent. Rather than a dualism of
antagonistic opponents caught in a cosmic war, we are reminded
of the easy relationship between day and night, chaos and order,
male and female. This is the concept of Yinyang, comprised of
yin, among whose complex etymology we are offered the shady
north side of a hill, situated alongside *yang*, its sunny south.
The opposites form a whole.

This metaphor might help us view the Left and Right of the
political spectrum without descending into hostility. It points
to the importance of dialogue, a two-sided exchange from
which some form of wisdom might still emerge. We can maintain our partisan or centrist affiliation while appreciating that

what resonates with us is only part of a whole. Politics should be, after all, about balancing the affairs of state rather than battles of rhetoric and power. It seems a very distant world in which our governments might wish to explain the difficulties of navigating complex issues, strive for unison rather than division, and seek agreements across party lines. (The American philosopher Harry Clor espouses this unlikely ideal in his book *On Moderation.*)

Meanwhile, throughout much of the Ancient Chinese world view we see an appreciation of ambiguity and inconstancy. There is a notable deviation in the writings of the fifth century BC political philosopher Mozi, whose divine code prescribes clear delineations of right and wrong, a set of guidelines which one must follow to live well and avoid punishment. His stable framework rests more easily with us, as it allows us to make clear and rational choices as to how we should behave. But aside from his teaching, Ancient Chinese philosophy generally shows us a way – indeed *the* Way: the Tao – to navigate an unpredictable universe. It emerged during a period in which the great dynasties were waning. Upon this shifting ground the philosophies offered new ways for citizens' lives to find their feet.

Crucially, the Ancient East did not seem to share our fixation with the isolated, autonomous self, but preferred to see us as muddled beings in fluctuating, ambiguous relationships with those we encounter. Whereas we in the West are easily enamoured with the notion of being authentic, 'true to ourselves', even accepting of our good and bad parts, the Ancient Chinese tradition would prefer us to prioritize *better interactions with others*. It might propose that what we see as our 'authenticity' amounts to no more than a bunch of confused behavioural patterns into which we have fallen; we are better advised, through the observance of seemingly mundane rituals and attention to the details of our behaviour, to cultivate a certain benevolence – or *ren* – in our relationships. It is a very lovely idea.*

For me, the greatest gift of Chinese philosophy (as I understand it) is the wholehearted embrace of the ever-changing, fluctuating nature of our futures. The focus on the minutiae of

---

* Reading Will Storr's *The Science of Storytelling*, I was happy to see that the contrasting landscapes of East and West may have been responsible for this fundamental variance in thought: the hills of Greece would have separated people and most likely necessitated individualistic thinking and trading, whereas the plains and open spaces of the East may well have encouraged dialogue and cooperation.

behaviour in the present seems to echo the Stoic theme of attending to one's activity in the here and now. We are encouraged to forge an easier accordance with others, and to retain an openness to forthcoming opportunities. Thus, when we make decisions about our lives, we might choose to remember the open-endedness of possibilities-to-come rather than act as if our future is something we can fix. We can make choices based on *what will maximize future opportunities*. If we practise seeing life as a series of disparate interactions lacking a stable structure, we can elevate the importance of the connection points we generate now. In doing so, we might find ourselves more disposed to cultivate better responses towards others. Not simply for the sake of being nicer, let alone to 'network', but to shift focus from the 'inner self', which gets far too much press, to its outer aspects, which are fluid, and nurtured in relationships. Those connections spread to form a matrix which in turn represents the possibilities of opportunity, luck, love and meaning of which our lives consist. This web of relationships is far more likely to work for us than a single-minded adherence to a specific personal projection. Life is ambiguous, complex and messy; we can at least look to meet its unpredictable nature with an open heart.

Finding synthesis

Accepting ambiguity might mean accommodating our personal Shadows in a world of conflicting viewpoints, battling egos and people trying to do their best. We can make a stand and take a side, but still welcome the nuanced truth found in those long grey stretches between black and white.

When faced with a question of true or false, we might look to see how both sides can be embraced. But the point of our appreciation of nuance is to deepen understanding, not to fall into a mire of conflicting detail and blurry indecision. So finally, then, we can keep our eye on possibilities of *synthesizing conflict*. Not in order to arrive at an alternative set of certainties, but to furnish ourselves with more mature and subtle understandings. We might achieve this by reminding ourselves from time to time of these two unnerving truths:

1. *We have grossly insufficient knowledge of the facts.* The ecology of information in which we find ourselves is polluted at every source. Whether it is our misgivings about our partner or our opinions on global matters, we are working from a hopeless privation of information. In personal matters, our projections,

defensiveness and complexes make it impossible to talk objectively when tensions mount. On a wider scale, when it comes to information sources regarding social and environmental matters, our situation is as hopeless.

We are far more likely to seek to align ourselves comfortably with our in-group (and against another) than we are to consider complex data on the topic at hand (even if it were available to us in comprehensible form). Moreover, when it comes to objectivity on scientific matters, we know that despite our best hopes for research, it is generally tainted by sponsorship and other financial incentives. Even if it were guaranteed to be entirely impartial, that would not solve our problem. For even the good information we receive through the media and our feeds is not unfiltered research data: it amounts to a curation of results that have been rearranged to serve a message. They have been repackaged and passed on by pundits, whose power over us will more likely come from *how they make us feel about ourselves* than the honesty of what they communicate.

To be wary of the reliability of the message under these conditions is not to discredit science, it is to continue the scientific project by valuing objectivity above all else. In these circumstances it is near-impossible for us to distinguish good information from bad. What is sincerely communicated may not be true, and even what is true may not be representative of the wider picture. Far more often than we like to admit, we simply look for what fits our pre-existing beliefs and disregard the rest. If that is uncomfortable to hear, it is because it creates a conflict with precisely one of those pre-existing beliefs: namely, that we are able to discern good information from bad and are less prey to cognitive biases than those around us.

2. *There is both signal and noise in our beliefs, and in those of people who oppose us.* It is very hard to truly listen to another's opinion when it contrasts with our own. From the moment their viewpoint takes shape in expression, we start to form counter-arguments and experience a rising frustration that makes dispassionate receptivity quite impossible. But from time to time we can remember: truth is being expressed there too, in some form. Our partner's radically different way of seeing the world is an honest expression of reality, formed principally during a unique sequence of childhood events and difficulties, and predictably at variance with ours. The political opinion we cannot stand to hear may be rabidly expounded, but it is likely to be a view of the world that is

partially true, like ours, and for that matter no less frightened, in-groupish and myopic.

Furthermore, we live in an age when our sources of information show each of us very different content, depending on how we already identify or where we live. Right-wingers browsing their social media during the Black Lives Matter troubles of 2020 would have seen videos of rioters ruthlessly looting shops, while Liberals would have been shocked by footage of police beating up peaceful protesters. Two very different stories. In the Netflix documentary *The Social Dilemma*, Justin Rosenstein, the co-creator of Google Drive, Gmail Chat, Face-book Pages and the Facebook Like button, gives us another vivid example of this kind of discrepancy in information:

When you go to Google and type in 'Climate change is . . .' you're going to see different results depending on where you live. In certain cities, you're gonna see it autocomplete with 'climate change is a hoax'. In other cases, you're gonna see 'climate change is causing the destruction of nature'. And that's a function not of what the truth is about climate change, but about where you happen to be Googling from and the particular things Google knows about your interests. We can no longer presume common ground and a consensus about world events. This is why the other side seems mad to us: they are working from different information.

There was a time not long ago when our news sources seemed monolithic, authoritative and trusted. It's odd to reflect how much we once craved *more* information on subjects of interest to us: there was ultimately less of it about. Somehow, we were happy to accept that the vastness and complexity of humanity's last twenty-four hours could be summarized in a handful of curated articles or reports from the studio. Then in the late 1990s came the first blogs, and Wikipedia a little later; soon old-fashioned journalism was all but crushed under the weight of information's democratization. The old behemoths started to look biased, elitist, or at best arbitrary in terms of what they chose to report. Newspapers seemed out of touch and were a day late with everything. At least the establishment had a budget: glossy production values allowed us for a while to distinguish between professional news and amateur. But with fewer technical and financial barriers to film-making, even that visual distinction has disappeared.

I've watched documentaries that have successfully turned

me from much of the meat market, but now films about dolphin genocide and the iniquities of the fishing industry leave me confused and guilty when I scan the weekly deli counter. I have no context in which to assess the damning information I receive about the slabs of salmon and tuna that denounce me glassily from the ice; there is no equivalent of peer review for these authored and passionate documentaries. When I read accusations of deliberate one-sidedness I wonder if such criticism is tainted by the financial interests of dark conglomerates, or whether bias even matters much any more. It seemed to matter when Michael Moore made *Fahrenheit 9/11*, criticizing Bush and his War on Terror: I remember the accusations of propaganda and the queasiness they produced in me after watching it. But now, partisanship is a given, and a lack of a strong authorial voice only has the old-fashioned and troubling effect of making us think for ourselves. All I have instead to guide me is how the programme made me feel, which means I am entirely in the hands of how shrill its tone was, how much it *seemed* to engage with conflicting viewpoints, and technical considerations such as the quality of editing. I am clueless as to how I should judge the fairness of the content. I turn from the tuna and consider the neighbouring arrangement of cheese with as much disquiet, aware that the next devastating exposé will target the violence and misery of the dairy industry. I glance hopefully at the veg, and then recall a report from Tel Aviv University in which researchers had recorded ultrasonic distress signals from tomatoes that were left unwatered or had their stems cut.

The result of this avalanche of modern information and the canniness of communication and marketing surrounding it has been a disconcerting lack of confidence in any information source at all. And we are left to respond to that perpetual mode of uncertainty with only anxiety or indifference.

In politics we can still dig deep and remember: the Conservative who wishes to consolidate the group against outside threat, and encourage growth with a hands-off economy, holds a part of the picture as vital as that of the Liberal who wishes to fortify the suffering individual and have the state support the weak. When worlds oppose on matters domestic and global, we might take an unusual initiative: to listen for truth rather than falsehood. That means depersonalizing the issue, which is not easy, and perhaps not entirely possible. But to genuinely listen, we must be happy to ask, *How is this true?*

We can also entertain a higher level of complexity. The idea of *dialectic* has permeated philosophical thought since the Ancient Greeks; it is identified with Aristotle and was given new life in modern times by German thinkers. The notion unpacks into the familiar triad of thesis/antithesis/synthesis, which describes a way of arriving at the truth from opposing viewpoints. Here is my view (thesis), there is your opposing one (antithesis), and if we pay attention to what is true in each, and how those truths might complement each other, we can arrive at a resolution (or synthesis). The effort taken to amalgamate both sides of the argument has then not only resolved a dispute but provided us with a new and valuable insight. And we have bestowed a favour upon the world by depriving it of an incautious pair of certainties.

With one less conviction based on insufficient information, there is one less battle being fought, one less offence taken, one less badly-arrived-at half-truth promulgated into the information environment. The move towards synthesis is aided by recalling that there is a charitable prerogative open to us, wherein we can presume best intentions in the face of an unfortunate or ignorant remark, presuppose that people are likely to let us down because they are suffering, and that they have priorities other than our own well-being.

So how might we reduce conflict and find synthesis in the broad and troubled mire of identity politics? The philosopher Martha Nussbaum has written extensively on the subject of channelling anger through a 'transition' into effective acts of political advocacy. In *The Coddling of the American Mind*, Haidt and his co-author Lukianoff suggest a means of diffusing unhelpful antagonism to make way for real change and fruitful persuasion. They point us to what they call a politics of Common Humanity rather than a Common Enemy. The former, historically, has been the approach used when communities have most effectively advocated their human rights. The idea is that when we draw attention to the plight of a suffering group, either our own or one that we care about, we resist isolating them by drawing a conceptual circle around them. Instead we can draw a line around *all* of us, emphasizing what we *all* have in common, and then point out where those among us are suffering. By contrast, Common Enemy identity politics, as employed during the recent post-Obama years, draws a tight circle around a community, points the finger at the bad guy *outside* it, and unites the community *against* him. This has of late become the mode of both political extremes.

The efficacy of the Common Humanity approach lies in the fact that it engenders the warmth of fellow-feeling, to which we – especially those on the Left – are disposed to respond well. As the authors describe, the recent advocacy for same-sex marriage is a good example of such an approach: gay men and women demanding equal rights was not as effective a campaign as one that appealed on the grounds of the *universality* of love. This strategy is a good example of the kind of synthesis we seek. It brings people together to dissolve a conflict. It focuses on common standards of fairness and values shared by a nation, rather than an image of irreconcilably splintered factions within it (exaggerated by a narrative of crisis that can leave people on all sides alienated and bemused). It retains an important truth: that within a widely cast net of common humanity, we are not merely divided into the good and the bad but instead amount to a complex, messy, diverse and altogether ambiguous collection of people. It encourages compassion, and a more nuanced understanding of who we are.

Nussbaum's concept of Transitional Anger and the lessons of Common Humanity are designed to help people fight their corner more effectively: they show us how to better persuade when it comes to fractious matters. They are useful syntheses that have grown out of the attempt to bring conflicting worlds together while managing hostility. But it's also worth mentioning that those outside a community are in no position to suggest how those within should proclaim their cause: if we are excluded by the circle that has been drawn, it is primarily our job to listen and to draw larger circles ourselves.

We embrace ambiguity because it acknowledges the sentience of others and the staggering expanse of our ignorance. Its denial motivates a neurotic compulsion to reinvent the world in our image. Its acceptance, on the other hand, is the task of growing up.

FRICTION

A bit about technology

A dream kitchen is described in an issue of *The Better Homes Manual* from 1931 whose cutting-edge gadgetry reduces the number of steps involved in making cheesecake from the usual 281 to an unheard-of 45. Clive Thompson, writing many decades later for *WIRED* in 2019, reports on this unalloyed victory and compares it to the ethos of modern tech:

> Coders might have different backgrounds and political opinions, but nearly every one I've ever met found deep, almost soulful pleasure in taking something inefficient – even just a little bit slow – and tightening it up a notch. Removing the friction from a system is an aesthetic joy; coders' eyes blaze when they talk about making something run faster or how they eliminated some bothersome human effort from a process.

The principle that animates the multifarious algorithms of Facebook, Google and the rest of that creeping confederacy is explicitly *to remove friction* (and in doing so, to keep us happily on their platform). From the cockcrow of industrialization, the overpowering urge of technology has been to optimize, to increase efficiency. The engineer was humanity's 'redeemer from despairing drudgery and burdensome labor', offered the celebrated American engineer Charles Hermany in 1904. But software engineers wield a power that betrays a glaring, surely-too-obvious-to-mention fact: they are experts in neither ethical value nor what we truly need. Witness the 'Like' button on Facebook, which was introduced to bypass the friction involved in comment-writing: it allowed people not vouchsafed with the time to compose a leisurely response to simply record their approval with the press of a key. Another wrinkle ironed out. But look at the disturbing friction it created in its wake: a tsunami of Likes, and with it a nascent worldwide neurosis which has attached itself to how many of these cursed endorsements our posts are receiving. This of course in turn provokes strange new attention-mongering behaviours on our part as we seek to acquire more Likes, more followers, in order to keep these artificial, meaningless, unsatisfying relationships multiplying at breakneck speed.

The old-fashioned sharing of vulnerability – the true, evolutionarily wired basis of friendship in our world of touch and flesh – has found no home in this virtual sphere. The pronouncements and images we see and share promote narratives of enviable and unblemished success. And so we must expect the Shadow form of our evicted vulnerability to loom and take its revenge. Hence, along the way, we read of unprecedented levels of depression and even suicide among the young – those who have sought consolation in a synthetic world from which emotional honesty has been barred. Banished friction has found its way back into the mix, fortified into its most distressing form.

Among many now gaining a voice on this topic is author and entrepreneur Judy Estrin. She warns us of the dangers of the unchecked prioritizing of convenience by the corporations who control our tech experience. She wrote in her 2018 article for the online journal *Medium* (the piece itself issued with a gentle heads-up that it'll take '12 mins to read'):

'Gamification' and 'growth hacking' have become coveted skills. The mantra is 'make things frictionless'. Automate everything. Value the number of connections over depth of interaction. Employ ever more sophisticated psychological techniques and minimise obstacles to enticing and retaining users. All barriers to ingesting data and to on-boarding or distributing content, ads, or marketing campaigns are removed . . . but missing are the checks and balances needed to protect us from ourselves and impede those who use these tools against us.

The birth of the Internet was a dream of democratization and self-expression. Now, as market forces take our hand and guide us along the paths of least resistance, and as information is disseminated according to outrage rather than truth-value, Estrin laments, 'we did not anticipate the erosion of democracy'.

If the explicit urge to remove friction has been with us at least since the invention of the wheel, then perhaps we should just roll our eyes and see this as more of the same. After all, something in us resonates with the experience of efficiency. The aligning of our time and environment with our wishes is normally a source of pleasure, and seems to do wonders for our self-worth. How satisfying it is when we find shortcuts in our lives that let us go about the business of being ourselves without encumbrance. For example, to write these opening chapters, I have found a circuit of cafés and coffee-shops on Manhattan's Upper West Side which affords me a surprisingly satisfying daily routine. I wake up late around ten (don't judge, the show sends me to bed late), dress from a conveniently limited palette of clothes, gather books and laptop into a back-pack and head to Café Luxembourg for their exemplary avocado on toast (arriving at 11.15, moments before they stop brunch). From there, onwards to one of two places where I can get proper coffee and, later, lunch while I write; then home for the comforts of a familiar bathroom before heading to the theatre to perform. The walks between locations, untroubled by the friction of choice-making in a foreign city, are buoyant with a sense that I'm at my best: I've *nailed it.*

A certain dose of automation relieves us of the burdensome resistance of the everyday. In its place, and paradoxically a result of that very mechanization, something that feels like a *fuller* version of our human selves emerges to the fore – we are someone who is *getting things done* – and our souls swell because they are better aligned with the story we like to tell. Stripped of pedestrian sub-plots, we confirm a broader tale of flattering, unencumbered agency and authorship.

But there's the rub: these minor daily automations are *our own*; we author and sanction them. They tidy up our experience, minimize stressors, and elevate our sense of self to fit the image of it we carry, for better or worse. Likewise, when we use a tool in the interests of efficiency, we are normally serving our own ends – to mow the lawn or to spiralize a courgette. Although in other contexts, it is the very presence of friction that can help us find our better selves. For example, when well-meaning relatives eradicate all risk from the life of a frail parent to protect the latter from the daily dangers of bumping into things or falling, they are likely to erode all sense of agency rather than enhance it. To prioritize extending life over preserving its quality is to gradually erase all forms of friction, and with them, meaning and joy.

Furthermore, when we unknowingly submit to the algorithms that coax and shepherd our online selves, we jettison our own values for the agenda of hidden market forces. This will never be in our best interest, because those vehicles would ultimately like us to become addicts, and addiction never serves us. Our online experience aims to keep us hooked: watching YouTube as it slides us algorithmically towards videos of conspiracies and outrage in order to extend at all costs that

ALLERGIES GOT PICKED UP FOR

ANOTHER

FUCKING

SEASON.

precious commodity, our *time spent on site.* Our time spent in a world without a moment's consideration of the quality of our experience there. Tristan Harris, co-founder of the Center for Humane Technology which was behind Netflix's *The Social Dilemma* documentary, points out the frictionless way in which YouTube's diet videos, appealing primarily to young girls, eventually segue into those that promote anorexia as the platform's recommendations list persists in its uneasy counsel. 'Automating recommendations is cheaper than paying human editors to decide what's worth our time,' he wrote in a 2019 *New York Times* article called 'Our Brains Are No Match for Our Technology'. He quotes Edward O. Wilson, the Harvard professor and father of sociobiology: 'The real problem of humanity is the following: we have Paleolithic emotions, medieval institutions and godlike technology.'

Technology has expanded wildly in the decade since Wilson gave us those words, while our Palaeolithic brains remain very much as they were. When I meet Tristan for dinner at an otherwise empty Italian restaurant in New York, I am struck by what it means to be dedicated to saving the world from itself. He is softly spoken, compassionate and convincing, and in committed pursuit of his cause: that of realigning technology to be compatible with our values and sense of meaning. He tells me how he has repeatedly been included in the highest-level meetings for global emergency matters and is woefully struck by the absence of what we all presume must be the case: that in such rooms sit informed adults conceiving plans and making conscientious decisions. Instead, he says with a sigh, it's just empty talk and face-saving – working out what to say next to the public. As we discuss the cognitive trick that leads us to imagine someone else is going to take care of a crisis, he knows there exists only us – him and you and me – to bring about these urgent changes, to take the sins of the world on ourselves. And after talking with Tristan over a series of brunches and strolls during my stay in New York, it seems those transgressions weigh heavily. For a moment, as he consumes his supper of soft salmon and salad in the vacant late-afternoon venue, a hint of the numinous glimmers and recedes behind his brown beard and slight frame.

The value of friction

To develop our muscles, we strain and sweat and lift weights that are uncomfortable. Friction and struggle lead to growth. For many, such as the chap I have just repositioned myself to view more comfortably from this coffee-house, such Herculean efforts at the gym seem manageable. It is generally less easy for us to apply the same ethos to our mental well-being. In that realm, we are experts at shunning adversity: we avoid stress and seek easier forms of fulfilment. To this end, we have been seduced by convenience.

But is it frictionless expedience we truly wish for? Let me point you to a thought experiment from American philosopher Robert Nozick. Imagine a machine which gives you a lifetime of whatever pleasurable experiences you desire. These experiences feel completely genuine, in the manner of a sustained and very realistic dream. You merely have to lie unconscious on a bed, get plugged in by a nurse, and enjoy the illusion of a wonderful life. You can even pause to reprogram it whenever you like, in order to map out whatever experiences you wish to have next. The question is this: *would you prefer the machine to real life?*

Maybe, just for a moment, we might. But then something in us surely baulks at the idea of a prolonged existence of entirely illusory pleasure. Because nowadays we tend to equate happiness with a type of mood, the reasons may not be obvious. We may well be tempted to plug in for good if our current life is unhappy enough. But perhaps we want more than a state of euphoria or frictionless ease. That is the dystopian psycho-pharmaceutical solution of Aldous Huxley's *Brave New World*: a drug, Soma, which has been created to keep us happy all the time. What is missing from this artificially maintained vision of happiness?

Meaning certainly seems to be absent. We know that the induced experiences will ultimately be hollow. The stories we conjure to get through life demand meaning – a way of making sense of existence – and it appears to be this that we value most of all. Many of us describe our lives as happy even when we are *feeling* down; in doing so we are repositioning our criteria for what matters most at a level *higher* than a temporary mood. Those who can no longer identify any meaning for themselves are usually those who opt out of life altogether.

A life plugged into an experience-machine or high on Soma does not offer this real-world value to the user. Neither does it offer *growth*. If meaning demands a story to be told, then it also requires tension, which is a form of friction. Growth demands tension too, even more so. We cannot grow (and in turn find meaning) unless we incorporate tension and anxiety into our landscape of acceptable emotions.

We could, of course, configure Nozick's device to create the *illusion* of growth and meaning within the program, but still the question persists: would we choose that over the real thing? Hooked up via the skull cap and electrodes that deliver fantasies directly to our pulsing brains, we would never find ourselves truly at odds with the world. As a team of attendants periodically turned us and attended to our hygiene, we'd just smile feebly – an echo of a far-off world in which we were each finding love.

While writing this, my gaze is drifting back and forth from the neat rows of text on my laptop screen to the scene through the wide front window of Bluebottle Coffee, Upper West Side, Manhattan. Across the road is the grand stone flank of a bank; in front of it a blue truck selling hot breakfasts. El Chiauteco B reakfast & nch, it declares: a door, having been slid ajar, has broken up the normal flow of signage. On my side of the street:

two closely parked cars, a green trash can full far beyond its brim, passing poodle-crosses woolly and attentive to their owners, the similarly hirsute homeless, and urgent men with phones clapped to their ears. Closer still, what appears to be a red Henry Hoover, though no doubt named differently here, abandoned and separated from the hose that lies adjacent and forgotten, curling thick and pubic on the frosty sidewalk. *Pubic*, Jesus.

That earlier thought of a frail parent had drawn me into the scene outside, and a daydream about my father. Currently he is deferring to a staggering list of indispositions including but not limited to a double whammy of early Alzheimer's and vascular dementia, low-grade blood cancer *and* prostate cancer, kidney disease, anaemia and diabetes. This once active man, who spent his life coaching swimmers, today feels depressed and useless, a burden in a frictionless world that has shrunk to the distance between armchair and bed. Now, underscoring this thick fog of cheerless fancy, the stringy strains of Richard Strauss's *Four Last Songs* stream into my head through my AirPods Pro, a noise-cancelling earphone set that annuls the background chatter of the busy coffee-shop and presses into its place the congested and claustrophobic silence which I imagine descends before drowning.

And then abruptly, through said earphones, the airborne articulations of Felicity Lott are curtailed mid-*Abendrot* by the less soothing vocal assertions of Siri: 'TEXT FROM CHRIS, HOW MANY THUMBS IS THAT OUT OF?'

The sudden, surreal, mis-intoned intrusion startles me. It takes a moment to assemble it into cohesion. Chris, a friend, had texted earlier to ask how I was finding those new AirPods. I had replied positively but curtly with two thumbs-up emojis before closing my phone, as I was eager to settle into writing. This is his reply to my unbecomingly terse review, now dictated through the very same device about which he was enquiring, rendered in the cold, dead voice of British (male) Siri. *How many thumbs is that out of?*

A further unwelcome triumph of technological expedience: Siri can now punctuate those rare moments when you catch up with yourself staring out of a window, by aggressively dictating a text into your brain and sinuses. I am no longer even required to pick up my phone to check a message. I remember that the Scandinavian name Siri, short for 'Sigrid', means 'Beautiful Woman Who Leads You to Victory'. A welcome safety feature while driving and perfectly turn-offable if I paid more attention to my phone settings. But as I retreat into the enduring private space wherein my awareness has until now remained my own, I shudder to find it commandeered in the holy name of Convenience.

My flat white, which I see has quietly collapsed in on itself as I was typing, is a sweet-sour emblem of the frictionless advantage of which I daily avail myself. From the plight of the far-away Ethiopian bean-pickers, through the virtuosity of local downtown roasters and finally to the bearded, lumbersexual barista who tugs and coaxes his 3-Group Marzocco to its point of acrid yield, it's all coming up roses for me. But at least the choice to have a coffee was mine. Probably. I head out on to Amsterdam Avenue, emptying the cold cup down a sink near the door.

SUFFERING

Never have we been better advised to be suspicious of the prioritizing of convenience. It can misfire so badly when it is born from a desire to hook us to a product rather than a sensitivity towards our needs. It carries in its Shadow a damaging friction crueller than the one it seeks to destroy. When we are not bumping up against incompatible or abrasive information, we are not learning. We are neither growing nor becoming strong. Unpalatable information teaches us something about the ambiguity of the world; in the same way that those areas where we clash with our partners are commonly the fertile soil where we ourselves need to grow.

How might we, as inheritors of our Western mode (and unsure how comfortably we sit with that of Ancient China), face the frictions and disturbances of the world? Some young people, for example, now presume themselves to be delicate and even in physical danger when challenged by the friction of inconvenient ideas. And such delicacy has a habit of assuming authority, in the same way that the less secure partner in a relationship tends to be the more controlling, as the other learns to tread carefully and cater to prickly sensitivities. The Stoics, by means of contrast, taught us the fortitude that comes from only looking to control our own thoughts and actions – the only things we *can* control – and choosing to live peacefully with whatever else befalls us. The mistake, they suggest, is to try to manage things we cannot, which guarantees frustration and the sense of disturbance they were keen to circumnavigate. Sage advice from a people who knew of warfare and terror. *You are not fragile, you have all the resources you need*, they would say; and *it is not the world's responsibility to protect you, it can only be your own.**

-----

* Before we roll our eyes at a bafflingly delicate younger generation, we might take a moment to recall our own responsibility. We did our best, but many of us, steeped in a culture saturated with therapies and self-help, protected our children from ever experiencing failure. As a generation, we ensured everything was defined as success, guaranteeing passes and awards for all; we may well have disproportionately helped with school work and over-managed their friendships and formative years. We largely denied them the opportunity to learn resilience. In effect, our own worries became a breeding ground for poor coping skills, a sense of entitlement,

Without this Stoic wisdom, what is our default mode? We recreate what's familiar, we seek to control with little discrimination, and we distract ourselves with entertainment. To these ends we repeatedly find partners who create for us the same family dynamic we knew as children; we baulk and manipulate when they do not; we develop addictions and try to build futures that continually elude us; we binge.

These daily measures that we put in place to ensure our world conforms to the story we prefer to tell about it, or to distract ourselves when it does not, are the familiar strains of being human. Remember Schopenhauer's diagonal line along which he plotted our life: the pull of our aims and strategical manoeuvres in one direction and that of blind Fortune in the other, correcting the gradient. The undulating line that climbs and dips along its $x=y$ diagonal will bring us to an occasional peak: a great new job, a kind and beautiful new partner, a vibrant

---

and a deeply anxious generation (who would go on to discover social media). But then, wait – were we not ourselves the offspring of parents who grew up in households darkened by the shadow of war, which enforced a leathery resilience at the expense of emotional subtlety? And so it continues, each new wave guided by fine intentions and broken compasses.

lucky streak in the face of life. And it appears in those moments that our strategizing and goal-planning have royally paid off, and while we modestly deflect praise, we inwardly congratulate ourselves on our magnificence. And then, on cue, Fortune reveals her hand. A lump on a loved one has leaked evil to her lymph-nodes; your phone has been stolen. In obvious and subtle ways, we are let down and our plans vanquished.

The Greeks knew it: life is tragic in its very structure. The *hubris* or pride that causes us to overreach ourselves will only invite the humbling response of Fate. Likewise, the Buddhists saw life as *dukkha*, which is often translated as 'suffering', but also incorporates a sense of impermanence and inevitable change. The Christian tale of life's suffering is inherited from St Augustine, who articulated to our collective unconscious the notion of Original Sin. They must be on to something.

Now let's sit with that for a moment. Sit in its *friction*. None of these schools of thought is telling us to despair. Each reminds us of our profoundly flawed nature in order to point towards a transcendental solution that might release us from its grip. We may not be especially attracted to the teachings of Buddha, or Christ, or know much about the Ancient Greeks, and so their particular answers might elude us. But a truth has been articulated for thousands of years, and with it a moving note of hope.

Despite all our attempts to distract ourselves, despite how frictionless we have grown to expect our world to be and how predictably we imagine our futures will fall into place if we plan well enough, a gravitational inevitability still drags us towards a centre that is difficult and heavy. We feel its centripetal pull not just at times of crushing tragedy, but also in the mundane moments of immovable sadness, when we are unable to sleep, gorged on Netflix, next to our partners and profoundly alone; or when we hover late in the evening by the living-room light switch, and a faint nausea stirs us as we notice our chairs and cups and objects are still arranged dumbly as we last left them, and will be so tomorrow.

We feel it in the ache of sadness yielded by love. A romantic relationship, once we are properly enveloped within it, has an undercurrent of tragedy. The note of despondency sounds as we realize every day that we are a disappointment to our partner; that they are too in return; that they are crueller to us than anyone else, and we to them; that our friends are kinder and seem to understand us better; that an active sexual life is no longer promised for the future; that we may not be desired; that something has silently left the room and will not return.

I am asked a lot, out here in New York, how it feels to be doing a Broadway run. The required answer is to describe perpetual and uncontaminated excitement. And it has been huge fun. New York sparks and fizzes with a galvanic charge, and at rare moments, performing a Broadway show seems to take that voltage and place it in my hands, streaking light between my fingers like the Tesla-gorged girls of those old Coney Island Electric Chair acts. Moreover, a tradition along the Great White Way decrees that famous actors and the like who are attending the show usually come round to say hello afterwards, and thus many nights have seen me frantically stuff socks into a drawer and greet the great and the good. At times this chimera of fluff and sparkle even resembles the self-aggrandizing snippets and curated snapshots that comprise my social media feeds.

Sunday and Monday nights, however, offer no shows, and the sudden appearance of an early, empty evening in my production-provided apartment brings a baffling unpreparedness for the lack of company or excitement. They can be surprisingly, desperately lonely. In London, to decamp to my library for the evening with a book, a Scotch and a recalcitrant beagle-basset is a jealously protected treat I secure with stealth and guile, ushering my partner from the house with encouragements to see the world and explore. Now, I'm dogless in a white-walled flat, thousands of miles from home, and I haven't charged my Kindle. I've forgotten to make plans, it's too late to do work, and a first-night gift of dark Japanese whisky is looming from the side table, hinting at unsettling prospects. I don't even have the company of a partner from whom I can have the pleasure of separating myself.

Three months into a run and it's of course natural to pine for home. In my afternoon coffee-shop, writing in a busy, creamy world of frothing milk, frolicking babies and mashed avocado, I cannot locate the strange sadness I know will return if I don't plan for these shadowy, showless evenings. I put it down to missing my man, whom I cannot call in those dark times as he'll be curled up asleep in our big London bed, his head plopped off the pillow like a babbie. But I am more disturbed by the suspicion that I am suffering from a disappointment in being left truly alone with myself, which has rarely unsettled me in the past.

None of this is a tragedy, and it would be perverse to expect sympathy (*oh, does your provided New York apartment only have white walls? It sounds like a nightmare*). But I am struck by how the fun of my time out here is conjoined to its assured reverse, and how impactful is the sudden absence of distraction. Distraction is the dazzling circumference of the circle: for me, it is performing the show, book-writing, *The Crown*, occasional dinners and drinks, sometimes buying clothes, days taken up with PR work. It is drawn wide around that dark centre whose pull I discern when none of the above is available and even the pale prospect of a blue-glowing e-Reader only accentuates a crushing, lonely failure of a night.

When the evening is like this, how comfortably isolation seems to fit us. How snug the sadness, how well tailored our particular worthlessness. We yearn for connection more than further distraction; the thought of watching another episode, or a fresh round of checking phone apps, only darkens the mood more. At least if we're in our home country we can scroll and flick through our contacts wondering who might be around, who might offer a glimmer of hope, which of our old cohorts' company will be less distressing than our loneliness, as if it were possible to summon the effort actually to go out and meet anyone.

You and I are then turned to that lumbering giant which accompanies us at all times: *our private life*, which leers back, embodying all our embarrassing, cheap, clumsy truths, and shines disappointing daylight on our mysteries. Unable to summon even the energy to sit and read, now that all objects in the room have withdrawn and return only a mocking acknowledgement of their over-familiarity, I descend into a kind of blank stare, which provides at once the warmth of settling into the bosom of *something*, and at the same time, as I view myself from without, a horror at my inertia.

But it is here at this central, seemingly starless spot, I think, that we might identify a profound and surprising consolation.

The centripetal point

Our moments of misery, whether unexpected catastrophes or twilight intimations of the tragic structure of our biography, reveal to us the precise *weight* of life. The stubborn friction we feel as we cannot create the world we want, the sense of grinding halt as we stare into space and our eyes moisten for no reason our adult selves can discern: these moments reveal the true poundage of existence. And as we face our silent giant, it is almost impossible to imagine that we are now at the centre of things, that we now feel the true heft and business of life, that despite our desire for nothing but a return to bed, we might actually be *most alive*. Alive, that is, in the sickly, fearful distaste we feel for ourselves, which has seeped into the fabric and contours of our living room and now uncolours the scene, reducing our busy world of things to a membrane draped over drabness. But it is precisely there that we might catch a glimpse of life without distraction. Which means, *it is universal.* We are, at those moments, most profoundly connected to those from whom we feel inconsolably removed.

If we take a feeling of personal sadness and nudge it into a more charitable acknowledgement of the universal, we transform it into *melancholy*. Melancholy leans into the tragedy of life, but refuses to render misfortune our private property, or ourselves blameworthy. It allows our capacity for unhappiness, the fall-out of Fortune's inevitable friction, to find its resting place without destroying us. The alternative would be an inward-directed sadness, which takes a healthy regret for our beleaguered place in the world and muddies it with a conviction of personal failure. Melancholy does not try to resist the sadness, in fact it deeply feels its appropriateness, but it kindly directs our awareness out into a world teeming with fellow creatures, each of whom, irrespective of outward success, face their private dark moments and are stalked by their own lurching monsters.

When we *personalize* our sadness, we may have fallen for the primrose promises of the snake-oil industry, and started to believe that through a lack of foresight, planning and self-mastery, we must be responsible for our failures. A grinning culture that assures us we can force fate into submission by personal effort will always point us to an equally personal failure when it inevitably reneges on its slippery pledges. At that point, like the faith-healer, it shrugs, proclaims it has nothing else to offer us, and blames our lack of faith. Naturally, a veil descends, and we suffer in silence. Our pain itself becomes a secret, because its roots connect it to a private place. Healthy melancholy may not fully cheer us up, but it extracts much of the poison.

The loneliness and tragic nature of romantic relationships, the fact that we are to be forever misunderstood and hectored by the person we are choosing to spend our life with – this too is transformed into common property, the correct weight of love. Viewed as an inevitable symptom of our common lot, we see it is neither our unworthiness nor our terrible misjudgement that has led to this impossible situation: it is merely the nature of two beings engaged in the implausible task of sharing their lives with each other. Good humour and self-forgiveness may turn out to be a better response than a continuous suspicion that you should be with someone else. The incessant hyper-sensitivity and bickering might mean that love is properly and appropriately in place. It may be difficult precisely for the reason that it is there to slowly and somewhat painfully transform us into better versions of ourselves.

Something magical happens when we reposition our perspective in this way. Unlike mere sorrow, melancholy does not seek to devour itself but instead it reaches out – it *yearns*. In this yearning (and the best melancholy music provokes this most clearly), desire, unknown when in the grip of depression, is reignited. When we acknowledge life's inevitable periods of tragedy and invite the consolation of commonality, the sense of our suffering stretches wide across the surface of the planet, through the hearts of those who brush past us on rainy streets, those whom we see alone through a window, and those who live and endure on the other side of the world.

It pushes too at the edges of our comprehension: we might vaguely acknowledge that we all share in pain, but the image of quite what that means, extended across so many people and back and forth across time, is a far harder image to contain. In losing something of the specificity of our selves into the generality of the human, we are moving into the queasy realm of the boundless. At this point we can emerge from the dense woods and meet with an expansive and surprising panorama: that of the ancient Sublime.

The Sublime

Our modern use of the word suggests a kind of impeccable bliss. A sunset, a symphony, or a certain style of stupor. There is an enervated, narcotic air about the word which is at odds with its original sense. It derives from *sub* ('up to') and *limen* ('threshold'), and thus evokes a sense of the mind being pulled to the limits of what it can experience or comprehend. For that reason, the Sublime was distinguished from the merely Beautiful in that the former was thought to contain a sort of terror. *Awe* is a helpful notion to more accurately conjure the mood.

The word 'Sublime' was first presented around the first century AD by the philosopher and critic Longinus, to describe a style of rhetoric that overwhelmed its listeners. There is a sense of conflict, even violence, central to the idea; as the notion expanded and waned in later centuries, this dramatic element remained attached. Around the eighteenth century we in the West became particularly interested in how the natural world, in its vast and overpowering forms, offered us the experience of this capitalized Sublime. The worlds of painting, poetry and music grew captivated by the concept, and the resulting Romantic movement was drenched in the project to sublimate oneself into the grand swell of Nature. The Irish aesthetician and politician Edmund Burke wrote extensively about the Sublime around that time, drawing on these components of fear and trembling: he conceived of the Sublime as an emotional state characterized by a combination of *terror* and *distance*. Its exhilarating aspects could be explained by the fact we have stepped back from something that would be 'alienating and diminishing' were we to get too close. A certain remoteness from otherwise dangerous mountains, for example, gives them an aesthetic quality that brings pleasure, but one that is inseparable from the lethal potential of being caught among their treacherous and overhanging rocks.

We seem to absorb into ourselves something of the greatness

we perceive, Burke felt, as we experience the Sublime. In other words, although we are overwhelmed and diminished by it, we also swell in order to accommodate its size. We wander the Alps with Wordsworth, through his *Prelude*, finding that the mighty Sublime is not to be discovered in Nature as much as in the 'unfathomed vapour', the 'awful Power' of our own imagination. When we consider the stars on a clear night, we might feel the sweet aggrandizement which paradoxically attaches itself to how small they make us feel. We shrink and lose ourselves in something bigger, and thus we feel ourselves expand. As Philip Shaw points out in his survey of changing notions of the Sublime, our *I* feels disoriented, as does our searching *eye*: neither is certain where to place itself as it encounters the dizzying infinite.

Here, then, is a vital point for us as we think about melancholy: we can enhance a sense of self by first losing it. If something draws crowds of holidaymakers and summer day-trippers to sit and stare out at the ocean, it is surely the stirring of the Sublime – a drawing out of the self into the infinite. Our *I* darts, unfocused, here and there upon the surface of the sea. At the beach on a clear night, we have felt it travel in search of starry constellations, crossed by sepia gulls picked out by pier and promenade lights, as our yearning soul slips its moorings and sails free.

A merely beautiful object gives us pleasure but perhaps little more; it is unlikely to exhilarate in the same way as the Sublime. When we look at a beautiful statue, piece of furniture, face or flower, we probably feel a satisfaction that everything is perfectly as it should be, and unquestionably in the right place. There is a sort of appropriation that happens – we might wish to possess the thing in some way, to line it up on a shelf, to display it for guests or for ourselves to marvel at. There is also, in most beautiful things, a lingering sense of transience, of finitude. A flower will die, the chair will break, and that beautiful person will wither and pass. We might say that beauty in its most striking forms seems to *ache*; it is often tinged with the sadness of a fleeting moment that will never occur again. The Sublime, on the other hand, seems to appropriate *us*, and its relationship to death is more explicit. We are beholding something frightening – kept safe by that all-important distance – which, if circumstances were different, might well be an agent of destruction.

One of the most beautiful endings to a film that I can think of takes place on a rooftop in Don McKellar's *Last Night*. The world is set to end at midnight, and some citizens of Toronto do what they must do in their final few hours. Among these characters, a widower, Patrick (Don), meets Sandra (played by Sandra Oh – the first time I'd seen her, and she was wonderful, as ever; they both are). We follow their story most closely: she is intent on killing herself, and he on spending the Apocalypse alone. The searing final moments, forever engraved on my heart, to the tune of Pete Seeger's 'Guantanamera' make me teary in a Manhattan coffee-shop years after last watching it. I won't spoil the movie for you, but as the couple finally find a way to love each other in the blinding light of the end of time, their moment is searingly sublime. The distinct story of two individuals becomes universal and therefore infinite: it is the finding of love over all else; it is the pain and pleasure of un-avoidable entropy; it is beauty trussed and tethered to death. Where mere beauty keeps its Shadow side hidden, the Sublime, by contrast, reveals its fearful self in full.

The notion we are considering in this chapter – to lean into suffering and difficulty when they strike, and with melancholic appreciation rather than despair – guides us to something like this sublime state. Here, on the one hand, is the pain of our iso-lation and fear, as we look at our dumb possessions or our sleeping partner after an evening of bickering. But there, on the other, is that same burden felt by all, and over all time. A vast vista unfolds which connects us to all humanity. We might sense our beleaguered soul rise and swell as it transcends our petty individual case, while another part of us remains unavoidably fastened to our particular circumstances. The melancholic distance we gain from our suffering is Burkean – the safe retreat which spares us destruction.

If in our darker moments we shift our gaze to the vastness of universal melancholy, we might recognize our individual sadness for what it is, and partake in the blameless fallout of the human condition and the unavoidable weight of a tragic structure. We can draw on the mightiness of the boundless and claim it for ourselves. When life pulls us towards its difficult centre, away from the circumference of surface distractions, we become part of something universal. We realize our precisely *us*-shaped fragment of the ache of humanity. From this same ache springs vital growth, as well as all our creative triumphs: we only yearn, after all, when we suffer and can imagine something better for ourselves. Perhaps, then, we might let the ache sit, and make friends with it. Rather than fasten our sights on the circumference of the circle – on a new ambition, or the fulfilment of a new project – we might try out less ostentatious aims.*

With our view from the centre, we might notice that life is largely a catalogue of friction – endless embarrassments and failures to do oneself justice. It's enough to try and pursue something worthwhile and take responsibility amid one's mess. *That* is a noble aim. And as many times as we can, we might endeavour to gather ourselves into a fresh inner coherence. Fortified by these modest resolutions, applied to the best of our limited abilities, we muster a judicious dose of melancholy. And in that place usually reserved for fear and isolation, we can, through the quivering of the ancient Sublime, rediscover a powerful connection with the world.

---

* We could, for example, worry less about self-esteem. High self-esteem is known to no one but the painfully self-deluded; not even swaggering narcissists truly possess it. Their particular needs after all hinge on a fundamental *lack* of self-worth: we only need what we don't already have.

SHYNESS

When I reflect on that Broadway run, one of its most striking and unexpected aspects was meeting those celebrated actors and other luminaries who attended the show. As I've mentioned before, there is a presumption in the air that if there's 'anyone in' that night they'll 'come round' afterwards (I note the satisfying double meaning of the second phrase in relation to my act). Thus I found myself mingling with the Great and the Good, and even receiving the odd invitation to their homes.

Normally after a show I am buzzing with adrenalin and confident I have done a good job. If I have erred at the finale I may be kicking myself or wishing to kick others, but a mistake would have to be truly terrible to suppress the soft glow of post-show euphoria which usually sticks around for a couple of hours. And of course it's while I'm in this state that I will greet anyone who has seen the performance.

I've already mentioned that I can be a little shy. So to meet these stars in this rather elated mood is by far the best way of doing it. I might hug them when they come in, and I'm sure I'm generally charming and open and warm. But I am in the very comfortable position of having just performed a show which (I hope) they have just enjoyed, and between that unusual dynamic and the exhilaration of the hour, I'm far from bashful.

Rarely, however, have I had such an encounter whose details a day or two later I am not running over in my head and berating myself for being an idiot. A fool for sounding full of myself, for name-dropping about such-and-such who was in the night before, for not seeming interested enough in them, for *anything*. On rare occasions we might even hit it off, perhaps leave the theatre to get a drink, and swap numbers as we say goodbye. This only causes the anxiety to stick deeper and stretch more generously over time, following an unrequited text the following week when I suggest coffee.

One night, then, the show was attended by a couple most would consider American royalty. I was invited to a post-show dinner and against all my expectations I arrived in fine form, my bafflement at the situation hidden just well enough. I did well: I was completely charmed by them both, was pleasant and happy, and left feeling wonderful. I couldn't have made too much of a fool of myself as shortly thereafter I received a second invitation, this time to a small festive party at their house.

Now unfolded the Fear. This would be very far from casual Italian dining with me on top post-performance form. I had months to sweat this out. I was repeatedly tempted to decline but I knew I should do nothing of the sort.

On the long-awaited afternoon I arrived with a friend I had brought for company, certain as I was that I wouldn't speak a word to anyone else all day. The gathering was smaller than I'd imagined, strikingly friendly and informal. Slowly I began to feel more comfortable. When our host came over, his gift of making me and others feel at ease was extraordinary. To our hostess, on the other hand, I had barely managed to speak, other than to hand over an extravagant bunch of flowers I'd bought in a panic before getting in the car. The congenial atmosphere helped enormously, but some part of my brain remained wired and hyper-extended, like a cat being put in a bath. Then, later, approaching the dinner table from the buffet with my plated meal in hand, I searched for my name-card on the table and saw – with incredulity – that I had been allocated the seat next to the esteemed lady of the house. *Me?* It made no sense to me. *She has so many friends here!* I considered making a switch, but it wasn't an option. Instead I sat down; then she did the same; and for an hour and a half I found myself denuded of all charm, unable to maintain a conversation beyond a few pleasantries. A ghost of my former post-show self, I ducked low into my plate and ate turkey. The emphatic mantra *I DON'T KNOW WHAT TO SAY* repeated in my panicked mind loud enough to be audible to my neighbours on both sides. In fact, to my right was seated a guest (a senator, I think, or an ambassador; I wasn't sure then either) who would have loved to be where I was, and for most of the meal the two of them held an animated parley about politics that skimmed the crown of my bowed and chastened head.

The worst part is, I'm lucky if I even came across as shy. The trouble with being shy is that you seem anything but: more likely you will appear aloof, cold, or uninterested. It takes a sensitive type to recognize the fact that you're daunted and have worked yourself into a paralysing frenzy of shame. And it is shame: shame that you have nothing to contribute, shame that you must be a very disappointing guest, shame that you've been like this before.

Now, apparently almost half of us think of ourselves as shy. If that is anything close to true, it is worth penning a few words on the subject. I cannot claim that these thoughts have solved all my problems, and they were certainly beyond my grasp during that dinner, but since then I have found them helpful.

Firstly, we can untangle a few threads. Shyness is not plain introversion. I think of myself largely as an introvert (this is not as uncommon for performers as you might think) but despite broad assumptions about extroverts being better company, this isn't a problem. Since Susan Cain's 2012 book *Quiet*, we introverts have enjoyed a little more understanding, or at least a better language with which to understand ourselves. We prefer, Cain explained, less stimulating environments, and have a tendency to 're-charge' alone rather than in company, unlike our more outgoing colleagues. Introversion has no inherent connection with anxiety or fear, and may very well be rooted in genetics. Shyness, on the other hand, entails a fear of negative judgement. It amounts to a very common, everyday social anxiety. It can accompany both intro- and extroversion. There are calm and anxious introverts, composed or nervous extroverts.

Shyness can expand into *severe* anxiety, which I first came

across when watching videos submitted by potential partici-
pants for one of my TV shows. We had asked people with
crippling fears to describe their afflictions, and here on tape
was one guy, Nick, setting out for us the lengths to which he
would go to avoid any social encounter. What struck me about
Nick's tape, aside from the eloquence and readiness with which
he was able to describe the ghost of a life he seemed to live, was
how *likeable* it made him. Not the consequences of the anxiety
itself, as that would manifest in ways which I'm sure would
cause misunderstandings and seem anti-social. But when
recounted openly in this way, Nick's sheer vulnerability made
him impossible not to love. The irony of the situation was
striking. Here was this chap, convinced that the world found
him embarrassing in every way imaginable. But that very fear,
expressed without the added distortion of his avoidance patterns, returned only warmth.

I had noticed a related situation occur on stage. I might
invite a volunteer to join me, and find that the moment they
walked up the few steps and found themselves before an audience, they would become disruptive. Unable to hide, as Nick
had found ways of doing, they would become cocky, make too
many jokes, or try to undercut what I was doing. After a few

times of feeling uncomfortable, I realized that whenever this happened I had no cause for concern. The trick might fail, *but the audience hated the participant.* I needed only to persevere, politely tolerate my volunteer, perhaps permit myself one sarcastic comment at their expense, and the room would be squarely on my side. Which turns out to matter far more than the trick. Everyone who comes on stage, bar the occasional psychopath, will feel anxiety in some form. And when they simply let that anxiety be present, honestly and openly, two thousand people will warm to them in a second. After all, it could be any one of them up there.

None of this helped me during that dinner as I spooned sweet potato the very short distance from plate to arid, useless mouth. I could have said: *I get so nervous! You're all so kind and welcoming but I'm so easily intimidated . . . which is so silly given that I do that show every night.* Why didn't I? It would have been to deploy a valuable lesson learned from Nick. Maybe next time.

On the one hand, all the clarity of hindsight. On the other, the same old narrative confirming itself repeatedly throughout the afternoon: *I just don't do dinner parties, I shouldn't go to these things.* On subsequent nights, a compulsion to replay the entire event in the screening room I keep in my head, which whirrs to life during those dismal hours when the world sleeps.

The plea of *I just don't do parties* is an interesting one. It helps us distinguish between whether what we have is a naturally introverted personality, which should not be a problem, or we are suffering from shyness. The key question as we consider our social lives might be: *If there were no problem, what would I like to be doing?* If the answer to that question involves *things that I'm not doing now,* then we know where we have an issue. I'm not sure I'd like to go to many more dinner parties than I attend now. But when I find myself at one, I'd like to enjoy it more than I do.

Back to the shame. For some it is the shame of blushing, sweating or stammering that causes the problem to escalate. For others (like me) it is the shame that we have nothing to offer the conversation. Commonly it is a fear that a *lack* of something is going to be laid bare. Perhaps for that reason, self-help books on the subject tend to offer confidence skills and social tricks, but like so many confidence tricks they rarely make good on their promises. Or if they do succeed, they do so in the way those seduction programmes work: by reducing your interlocutor to a target, or a pawn which must follow certain rules. Neither of you, in that model, is acting as yourself, and whatever skill you may be learning, it is extraneous to your natural set.

And there's the rub: all the skills we need we already have in place. It is no coincidence that the people who suffer from this form of anxiety tend to be among the most empathic and sensitive conversational partners. In fact the very problem may stem from caring too much about what the other person thinks. So consider: how are you with your close friends? With the stakes so low, you can be everything with them that you could wish to be. You are, I'm sure, already possessed with tremendous humour, touching sensitivity and a personality that on a good day might even pass as winning. In those familiar situations, you have everything you need in place. I'm always impressed with friends who somehow manage to remain themselves when in company I would find daunting. It's as if the stakes have not noticeably risen for them. They continue to be fully recognizable as the person I know, which to me is already the best version of who they are. The problem for the rest of us, perhaps, is one of certain misrepresentations that now get in the way. The answer is not, I think, to add new skills that are lacking; it is to find a way back to what is already in place. It is *not* that we're hopeless in these situations, that we lack this or that social ability. The version of ourselves which comes to the fore with friends – *that* is us, perfectly formed, and all we need to be.

Another lesson, then, from the stage. It is very common as an actor or entertainer that *your* experience of your perform-ance does not match your audience's perception of it. This is a truth so obvious to any of us who work with a director (and foreign to those who do not) that it borders on banality. For example, during that Broadway run I had a week in which I messed up a routine three nights in a row. The nature of the piece meant that if I lost concentration at the start, the next fifteen minutes would lead nowhere, and I would have to fail with not one but *four* different spectators. The first time this came to pass, I realized early I had made the fatal mistake, in the slow-motion way these thoughts unfold in the back of the mind when one is facing an audience with a script to follow. As my mouth switched to autopilot, delivering the lines I had said five hundred times before (a terrible mode of performance), I was simultaneously, frantically, searching for solutions and escape routes. Could I justifiably start the routine again? What should I do? No answer suggested itself, and I was aware that

I was sweating. As two thousand people studied my every move, I felt my forehead prickle with moisture, along with the back of my neck. I continued as an automaton towards what would have been the first climax of the routine, made a clumsy guess, and failed. Silence from the crowd. No surprise. I moved on to the next spectator, wondering if the situation could be salvaged with a fresh round. But it couldn't, and once again I foundered. Then came a third miscarriage, before finally, after a substantial and excruciating crescendo, a further, final, damp fart of a failure.

During this fifteen minutes or so of horror I was convinced that I had become transparent to the audience. My experience was so very different from normal, so there was surely no way theirs could remain the same. Two thousand once-friendly eyes now seemed to bore into me, recognizing what they saw as a frightened, perspiring fraud. The routine finished, I sent the final participant back to her seat, cueing tepid and bewildered applause, and apologized for the abject mess of the routine. I continued with my script, the anxiety quelled a little, and twenty seconds later came a surprise. *The next joke got the same laugh it always did.* This meant they were back on track. *They hadn't cared.*

They had not cared. They had seen me struggle and fail, but they had not seen *me* in the way I did. They had not sensed my agony. Even if they had, of course, it would have made me more compelling, more human, like Nick. A trick failing, even a long one, early in the performance is not really a danger to the show. More important to an audience is how the performer deals with it. After all, 'Oh God, it's going wrong' could be an *electric* feeling to have as an audience member, as long as the performer doesn't make the mistake of handling it ungraciously – such as taking the common route of blaming the crowd.

Next night, I made the same mistake at the identical point in the routine, which was idiotic. The night after, the same again – inexcusable. But each time my anxiety level was lower than that of the previous show, because I knew that the audience were in fact on my side. I had developed a new relationship to the experience of failure and to the crowd: the realization that my fear of damning judgement was based on a complete misreading of the spectators' experience, and that post-failure they were more than happy to carry on as if nothing had happened, was deeply liberating. My private conviction of how I was being perceived had simply been wrong. It really *felt* like I was exposed as a fumbling amateur, but that reality was outvoted roughly two thousand to one. I had learned one of the most valuable lessons in twenty years of live shows.

If you are a performer, you usually have a director to let you know how your words and actions are reaching the minds of the audience. He or she is there to make sure the show is having the desired effect. Many times I have had one or both of my directors in, having left the stage convinced the show was a flaccid flop of errors. I've sheepishly awaited them, only to find, when they arrived at my dressing room, that they adored the show. And similarly in reverse: I've expected congratulations and been met with more than the usual number of notes for improvement. Even though there are auditory guides to how well you're doing – the sound of coughing, for example, usually signifies that you've lost the crowd – what one feels is happening on the inside has no automatic relationship to outside reality. Once you have a rehearsed performance in your bones, you might be dying up there but *no one knows.*

When what is going on in the private, offstage area of our thoughts is of so little import in comparison to our public words and actions, the key is to make sure, like a magician flailing with a trick three nights in a row, that we have a script of sorts to fall back on and see us through. Fraught internal machinations will catch up and calm down if the social situation improves, which it will, *when our words and actions are right.* So what are the right things to say and do? The answer: they are the things you say and do with people you're comfortable around. Draw from your own experience. Your answers are there.

Take, for example, small talk. No one enjoys it; everyone except the truly tedious is looking for a way out. It feels like a trap because we are unable to show ourselves: conversation is caught around the subjects of trivial things in the external world and we can contribute nothing about ourselves nor hear anything of interest about others. The best response, then, is to provide such a lifeline for yourself and your company, rather than to remain stultified by it. In the company of your friends, this would never happen. If one of them asked you *So how was your journey?* or *How long does it take you to put a show together?* or *How do you know Brian?,* your answer would rarely be straightforward and factual. You would give the information – *Ooh, an hour and a half* – but most likely you would tack on some personal information: *but Giles wouldn't shut up for the whole journey, and* someone *was giving me really helpful driving tips from the passenger seat which at one point made me want to swerve into oncoming traffic.* If there was really nothing to add, you'd quickly move on to another topic or ask something your-self. The reason why we find small talk so hateful is most likely *not* that we lack a skill for it or are no good with people. Per-haps you're actually *very* interested in people, and want to get to the juicy stuff but can't find a way out of the useless fact-gathering dirge.

A common difference between charismatic types who make you feel comfortable and those from whom you will walk away certain that you have wasted your time is that the former ask questions that bypass the specifics of, say, your job and quickly cut through to the things that connect us as humans. If you are introduced to someone as a teacher, what sort of conversation would you rather have? One about teaching, or one in which you are both laughing about a weird fear that you happen to share? Small talk feels superficial, and conversation can feel uninteresting, because it never ventures beyond the level at which you are immediately presented, such as that of a school-teacher. And likewise, if all people know about you is that you have a connection with Brian who is hosting the party, they will probably ask about the nature of that relationship. Your mission, should you choose to accept it, is *not* to get better at small talk, it is to provide an *exit* from small talk by offering a lifeline into comfortable personal territory and expanding options for connection. And if you do it gently, people will grab at it. *Brian? I met him at a friend's work thing. He taught me a trick with a glass of water, which I went home and tried and ended up drenching the dog. My son makes me do it for guests now. My son's a bit of a dick like that.* So many lifelines there for connection. *What's the trick? How old is your son?* Even, *What breed of dog do you have?* And then, as things progress, your specific son or dog will turn out to be not as interesting as, say, the ordeals or rewards of *having* children or pets – subjects which offer further possibilities for relatedness.

At the New York dinner party I was describing, the host, who was of a certain age, had a phenomenal habit of joining a group, putting his arm around the shoulders of one or two people and telling us about which bits of him were no longer working properly. Not a single question about our jobs, no attempts to 'make conversation', just a jump straight into the great levelling territory of human vulnerability from a man of towering social status. These words and actions were enormously effective and a lesson I have carried with me since. Yes he had huge charisma, but it wasn't complicated. *This was exactly what he'd do with his friends.* And as if by magic, I felt like I must be one.

All this was lost to me at the dining table, of course. I was twirling my wine glass and scrabbling for things to say that might be worthy of the company. The hosts and guests couldn't have been lovelier, and I was an immensely lucky boy to be there, to be in that house and in that seat. Every reason to feel embraced; every reason to feel inadequate. Occasionally an image would flash before my eyes: *I am here as a Broadway star. Broadway's a big deal here, the show is popular, that makes me interesting.* But it didn't stick. I wanted to ask, of this extraordinary woman to my left, *What's it like, being you?* It would have sounded mad, I'm sure. At best, an impertinent distraction from the fluent conversation she was having with the man next to me about things of which I had no clue. So I twirled and ate.

There is really no solution other than to take a breath and find something warm to say, something you'd say if you were feeling at ease. To dive in, despite the fear, with the right words and actions, knowing that the momentary anguish will subside. Waiting until you feel confident enough is not an option.

Those pernickety but useful questions from cognitive behavioural therapy tug at my ear. Ask yourself: *Excuse me, what's the worst that could happen? Be specific and realistic. What's the worst outcome? Would that scenario be so terrible?* Good, sensible questions. Then, be kind to yourself and say something nice.

If the feeling of discomfort were the extent of it, I could leave, dust myself down, have a drink and forget about it. But I never do: I am a seasoned enthusiast of the gruelling replay, which keeps me awake on subsequent nights, forced to watch those midnight screenings of *Mistakes You Have Made in Your Life* like Malcolm McDowell with his eyes taped open in *A Clockwork Orange.* The dinner I have described has remained a go-to recurring feature ever since. But I have noticed that since describing it here, the retrospective showings are less frequent. Perhaps there is therapeutic value in writing it out: not to further berate oneself, but to gain a little distance; to see where the silliness lies and charitably suggest solutions which draw on what one already has in place rather than new and foreign skills one is supposed to acquire.

Finally, there is a touching, misjudged purism about shyness: a difficulty in allowing oneself to appear flawed, average, unimpressive. But a readiness to appear unimpressive can be very appealing in the way we've discussed, in a way that a desire to impress never is. Coupled with this is our curious inability to appreciate that others too, by nature of being fellow human beings, will be suffering from similar concerns about inadequacy. If those people seem not to let their concerns show, it's only because they have grown accustomed to deadening the first flush of fight-or-flight rather than nursing it all evening. The purism is highly uncharitable, to oneself and to others. We clam up because we feel unimpressive, but *no one wants us to be impressive. They just want us to show we like them.* Our – my – attention needs sympathetic guiding from inside to outside. The good news is that us shy types, perhaps more than anyone, are particularly well equipped to offer such an empathic reversal of focus towards others.

THE SECRETS OF MAGIC

John, the general manager of my tours, telephoned me when I was in New York to ask a question I did not expect. Did I want a large iron Victorian safe in my dressing room? He was thinking of sending one over from London after finding it on eBay.

I hesitated, wondering what I'd missed. 'A safe? For keeping valuables in?' I said. What treasures did I own that would require such theatrical containment? And did America not sell safes?

'No – I mean, yes, a safe – but to keep empty. In your dressing room.'

'Empty?'

'An empty safe.'

Crash zoom to a mortar-boarded science teacher from the sixties, swinging the tip of a long pointer at an old map of the brain pulled down behind him. Hard cut to a tumbling flash of flume-ride through the serpentine interior of the brain's byways, and finally, accompanied by the sound of sparking electricity, a retro-biology-textbook animation of one crudely drawn neuron sending its chemical message to the eagerly waving dendrites of another. The connection was made, and it fizzed.

An empty safe. Theatrical magic is rarely the ready source of wonder it professes to be. Its mysteries tend to lack lasting resonance. This discrepancy between what it would like to be and the prosaic nature of how it commonly appears helps us understand why its secrets are so well protected. Sometimes they are beautiful in their simplicity, but most often they're ugly and disappointing. Jim Steinmeyer, a hugely respected designer of magic and theatrical special effects, once pithily pointed out – and here it is – that 'magicians guard an empty safe'. We make a play of protecting our methods not because they are in themselves of great value, but because the revelation of their dullness would most likely expose us as pantomiming fools.

Knowledge of Jim's phrase, I noted with surprise, had found its way to John. I was mesmerized for a moment, staring through the apartment window, superimposing upon the grey view of the park a looping movie of airport crew trying to heave the iron beast on to a plane. There was something deli-cious in the thought of such a profoundly inconvenient item being transported from London to New York for no good rea-son other than the pleasure of metaphor, so I agreed.

A week later, it was simply there. It had dutifully appeared in my tiny, antiseptic dressing room, incongruous and awkward like a gramophone in a hospital. And then, for the six-month duration of the show, the green dumb block occupied its place under my table – a ludicrous waste of much-needed space. But aside from serving as a palliative metaphor to soothe the strains of my own ego, I enjoyed the thought that it might puzzle and intrigue guests, as well as the crew and cleaners who came in. Locked and ominous, it remained empty for the entire run, waiting to be transported home at further considerable expense (I had only a very dim sense that I would ultimately be paying for a chunk of that).

If there are truly worthwhile secrets in magic to aid us in our search for consolation, we may have to look harder for them. I think they lie in our themes of how we meet each other, and the way we form and manipulate the stories by which we live.

Instructions: a card trick

To begin, sit down at the table opposite the lady who seems intrigued and not too drunk. Place your glass off to the left and introduce yourself. Remove a deck of cards from your pocket and hand them across to her to shuffle. While she fumbles and apologizes, shift a few objects on the table to make some space. Then retrieve the cards, snap them into a fan face-down before her, and ask her in the time-honoured way to pick one. Maybe she'll smile at the casually proffered flourish – a good sign – before she removes one and looks at it. Have her slide it back into the deck. As she does so, hold the deck in your left hand but mark the location of the incoming card with an imperceptible wedge of infringing fingerskin, in the way that you have learned from books and videos. Consider for a second how long it took you to become proficient in this invisible but all-important advantage, how many hours that took in front of the mirror in your bedroom, how it has expanded into a strange fascination with gaining the upper hand in a thousand tiny invisible ways.

Your actual hand is now a little tense and your smallest finger is locked in a strange position, so relax your wrist, nice and slack, so you're not signalling any strain that might pull her focus. Now, remember one of the first rules you learned as a magician: people will look you in the eye when you ask them a question. So look at her – not at the deck, look at *her* – and ask as you smile: 'Can you remember what your card is?'

She will look up from the deck to meet your eyes, and in that second as she does this, in that tiny shift as her gaze grazes your glazed dead eyes before dropping back down to the deck after a beat, bring your hands together to square the deck – a minor adjustment, the movement of a moment. Except *that* was the instant you used the benefit of your left fingertip's leverage to swivel the chosen card out from its place to the right, its journey hidden under the cover of the approaching right hand, as it swings safely around and to the bottom of the deck. That's if you're good at this stuff. So you don't know what the card is, but you know *where* it is (on the underside of the deck, the *face*), and now you can handle the cards as casually as you like. You can shuffle and throw them around if you like, as long as you keep track of that bottom card.

Note: a schism has opened up between the spectator's reality and *real* (your) reality. From now on she is working from a false premise, that her card is lost and you don't know what it is.

Even if she suspects you have some way of finding out (which she does), she doesn't know you already have it under your control. Her story is just starting, waiting for some action – *OK, so I've picked a card and put it back, is this going to be embarrassing? This guy is sort of cute but maybe weird* – but yours is different and already partway along its fixed track: *this woman is conforming to pattern, she seems convinced, her card is safely on the face ready to be palmed.*

As these stories continue in their different directions, the chasm will widen. The game is on. Her perspective will appear complete to her because she feels she's following everything closely. She is, but she can't follow *everything* closely. So she will take her cue from you: not necessarily what you *tell* her is important, but what you *cue* is important, what you show by your actions. And you hope she will delete from her memory whatever you demonstrate is unimportant, as she should.

One of the most delicious rewards of being a magician is realizing you have yourself been fooled by precisely this business of treating a vital moment as inconsequential. For example, during a trick, the magician cuts the cards on the table, but in picking up the bottom half to complete the cut, accidentally leaves one or two behind. He notices his error, makes nothing of it, picks them up and drops them on top of the deck and continues with the trick. I remember watching Guy Hollingworth, a modern genius of magic, do exactly that at an early point during a performance. I thought nothing of it – who would? It was a perfectly understandable slip: it can be hard to pick up a deck of cards from a table neatly. Yet when he later explained the complex method behind the miracle that followed, it turned out that that moment – the unnoticed misplacement of those one or two cards – was a beautiful piece of the jigsaw that in his hands contributed to a dizzying impossibility further down the line. It felt so *good* to have seen it and not seen it. Magic methods are rarely furtive: the best ones pass by right in front of you unnoticed.

Your spectator is following these cues as to what is and what is not important. She *thinks* she is trying to catch you out. But if so, she would insist on holding the cards herself; it wouldn't be too difficult. Or at least she could keep her gaze directed unwaveringly at them. Yet she cannot. Perhaps because the stakes are low: she also wants to enjoy the trick, knows there's a game to be played in which she has her allocated part. But perhaps also because she is a social animal and it turns out to be very hard to *really* try to catch you out, because that would be rude. So she watches closely, but she misses the walls of the restaurant and the bar transform into identical pieces of stage scenery, the customers become actors whom you might bring into the plot at any moment, and that the play is happening now and she and you are in it. Neither does it occur to her that she has been reduced to a perspective, a pair of biddable eyes on a meat-stick, an angle from which this trick must be performed in order to work. She has eliminated so much from her awareness in an effort to focus on *not* missing anything. She's certainly forgotten about that glass.

Forget the trick for a moment. She doesn't know it yet but she was derailed by a touching, predictable human response: she looked you in the eyes when you asked her a question. What happened? Maybe it's odd that she wants to respond to the enquiry: despite this strange context, in which she is going to try not to be fooled, she still wants to help by supplying an answer. When you asked the question, and because she is a living human being, she experienced a flush of serotonin, which relaxed her, and freed her up to find a response. Dopamine followed, which brought with it the 'fight or flight' response that comes when we look for a correct answer, but worry that we don't have one. And with these changes in her body happening at that moment, she was too busy to pay attention to cards or hands or the tiny obtrusion of skin.

This provides us with a sort-of understanding of why she misses the sleight, but it's not that interesting. What else is happening? What even is it to ask a question? *Do you even know?* (*Go serotonin! Dopamine! Fight!*) In itself, this question of *what is a question* has ruffled modern philosophers concerned with syntax and linguistics. They try to pin down what it means to be a question in terms of the answers to which they logically lead. But I'm not completely sure a question needs an answer. What even *is* a question. Is that one? It didn't have a question mark. If I type 'restaurants near me' into Google Maps, and I am reminded that there is a Thai place just over a mile from my house – was I asking a question? I gesture at an empty bar stool while making eye contact with the person sitting on the next one – am I asking one now? Instead of trying to define them in this way, only to feel them slip through our fingers, it might be better (I'm borrowing the argument of philosopher Lani Watson here) to look at them functionally: *what do they do?* They allow us to garner information. 'They are a subtle but indispensable tool, seamlessly weaving together our conversations, advancing our inquiries, and directing our attention to this or that.'

That's helpful, but I'm still not sure I'm where I want to be with this. I am looking for what is happening in that interpersonal moment. If you are after information (*do you remember the card?*) then you are, at that moment, *lacking*, and vulnerable. Not *truly* vulnerable, I know, because here the question is a ruse. But nonetheless she is compelled to respond to your need. She looks up because it's hard to picture something without lifting her eyes. If you'd asked 'How are you feeling?', she might well have kept on looking down at the cards as she warily provided an answer. But an answer that requires visualization encourages her to look up. So she does, seeking a point of connection, as well as any quiet qualifiers that might be supplied by your facial expression. Her ancestral history ensures that she observes your face to check the full meaning of what you are asking – the information not carried in your words. This information may define the dynamic of a relationship that has just shifted with your posing of a question. Are you asking because you're angry? Sarcastic? If she is going to let down her guard to answer this question, she'd better know she's safe. Your need – your vulnerability – has commanded her to respond. Your question has an immediately compelling power.

Your vulnerability and power are only part of the story: something in the other person holds each of you in the grip of both qualities. That's more what I'm getting at; but somehow this delicate dynamic seems to get going before you even ask a question. After all, what happens when we encounter a person on the street? What is that feeling when we make eye contact with a stranger? A brief, unspoken exchange. A silent assessing, or rapid calculating of needs and demands, of attraction or repulsion, of superior and inferior, as we cross paths, make room for each other, navigate past. Whatever is quietly at work here and barely noticeable would explode into consciousness if a stranger approached us to ask a question or make a demand. The question seems central to any encounter. And of course we can ignore questions and ignore people. But even in doing this we are still acknowledging them and the compulsion they trigger in us. And on the street, before either of us spoke or gestured, with the stranger's very appearance in our field of vision, did they not present some faint echo of demand that destroyed the world of which we were until that moment in complete possession, and over which we had full mastery? To one degree or another, our needs and theirs must now bargain with each other.

These thoughts bring me close to the Lithuanian philosopher Emmanuel Levinas, who saw the face-to-face encounter – and therefore the bedrock of our social existence – as fundamentally ethical in this way. In his mind, the history of philosophy has failed to appreciate the essentially social nature of our existence. We are neither fundamentally rational creatures, as the Greeks thought and we have continued to think more or less ever since, nor should we be reduced to the result of physical processes or swirling clouds of atoms. We are essentially *ethical*, because everything starts with the particular relationship between two individuals, and this entails a fundamental obligation. This core obligation will be tempered by the specifics of the interaction, such as the societal rules at play in that context. But first and foremost I am a being that is *responsible*. All else must spring from that seed of moral understanding.

It is that fundamental plea and demand that is driven by you with your intent to elegantly deceive your consenting spectator. She is not in any way a fool: she is responding reasonably and logically to the situation, and probably remaining more alert than ever to what might constitute deception. She has a touching, primordial need to understand and to be directed, to find her place in this interaction with another. The cues and obligations smuggled in by this encounter will soon result in a crisis, as her world loses its foothold, in as much as it has shrunk to the size of a few square feet of tabletop and the goings-on upon it.

I think again of the US race riots of 2020. Right-wing people seeing footage that damned with one story, those on the Left another. Such a human, natural, fundamental plea for information, a question to the world – *What's going on?* – answered in different ways, creating two different worlds, each incomprehensible to the other side. The great majority of us have no wish to seek nourishment from either of those starkly opposed realities, given that we live and breathe somewhere in between. We are a mess of concerns, groupish and selfish, compassionate and fearful, conventional and progressive. In this world of near-infinite information sources and the demonopolization of news, it is the very act of *asking*, as bare and naked as a face (Levinas describes our countenance in this way), that has driven us to occupy disparate, desperate worlds.

The glass. She has forgotten your glass which you placed on the table to the left as you sat down. You rearranged it while she shuffled the cards, shifting it nearer to her edge of the table, and close to the salt and pepper. She would be very surprised to learn that the apparently casual placing of the glass was very specific, well practised and part of the trick. She does not realize that even now her attention is being pulled up and away from it, so that it has disappeared from the story of things which might be important. She's forgotten that there's a glass there, but she doesn't know she's forgotten it, and in a moment when she sees her card under it, she'll feel she never took her eyes off it *or* the cards. But for now it's outside of the frame. And frames make things important: they say *look at this*, which means they also tell us what we can ignore. This is why we can create damage when we draw a circle – a type of frame – too tightly around groups of people.

So now, having just handled them casually and fairly, square up the cards in your hands, and say, 'Right, so if I spread these out, don't give away which one it is.' As you deliver that instruction, steal that bottom card into a left-hand palm. That's a straightforward move which you've done a thousand times, and depending on which version you use, she can be staring at the cards or not. But now you lean forward with the cards held in your right, across the table a little, the left having moved away and looking relaxed with its hidden card, and you know that her attention is now a little displaced as she processes the instructions you have just given. *OK, I mustn't give away the card, how would I even do that? And what's happening now?* Reach forward and spread the deck on the table in front of her from your left to right, starting halfway between where the glass is and her edge of the table.

As you start this spread, your forgotten left hand does a very natural and seemingly inconsequential thing: it adjusts the position of the glass a little further to the left to make the spread of cards more convenient. Her eyes, though, are following the large movement of the right arm and the expanding ribbon of playing cards that holds her focus – *there they all are, that's neat, I should see it but I mustn't react, where is it? I mustn't look too hard for it.* The left hand, meanwhile, in its small and efficient action, has not merely adjusted the glass. It has deposited the palmed, chosen card face down on the table next to the glass and then placed the latter on top of it. She should have missed this because she was watching the larger movement of the right hand spreading the rest of the deck, carrying her eyes to the other side of the table, and *a large movement hides a small movement* (your next basic principle). Even if she processed the left hand's movement peripherally, it would have appeared as a natural shifting of the drink to facilitate the spread, and thus soon forgotten.

'Don't give away where it is by looking at it,' you say boldly, allowing her to glance across a line of fifty-one indices, none of which is hers. But as your instruction only makes sense if the card is somewhere in that line, she presumes it's there. This may well not be the case if you stated it as fact, if you said *your card is in there somewhere.* Because then she might decide she wanted proof. *Hang on, let me just see* . . . So for the moment, to convince her that it's there, you use the power of presupposition. And she doesn't want to look too hard for fear she will give it away.

Both empty hands gesture as you speak, with the tone of someone now beginning a trick. 'OK, I'll show you this trick, but if it doesn't work, don't hate me, it's actually rather hard to do in this environment,' you say. The presupposition here – that the trick is only now about to start – is a clever ruse, given that you have done all you need to do. As far as you're concerned, everything that is required has been accomplished. But you now act as if you are about to begin. You are going to show, a little later, that her chosen card has vanished from the deck and appeared under the glass which now sits close to her.

At the moment the card is already there, bold as brass, unseen, as long as you can keep her mind and gaze occupied.

If the future story of the trick is only now about to commence, you are free to create the most impossible conditions for the miracle. So shift your chair, away from the left end of the table, so that later the glass looks out of reach, and invite her to watch carefully. *Watch carefully,* of course, means: *only pay attention to what I tell you is important. Pay very close attention to those important things so that you develop tunnel vision, and you don't notice that the glass in front of you has a card under it.* You placed it by the salt and pepper when you moved things around earlier, to slightly busy that part of the scene and make the card, when it arrived, less conspicuous. Because now you're going to ask her to pick up the other cards and you don't want her seeing it and picking it up too, thinking she missed one.

Ask her to gather them together, miming something like an accordion movement to illustrate. 'I won't touch them, I promise,' you say, now gesturing away with your hands, showing them empty again, the picture of innocence. 'Don't worry about making them neat. Just hold them in your hands and please watch mine. I'm going to touch your hands but I need to make sure I don't actually touch the cards.' And now hold her hands in yours, taking care not to touch the playing cards between hers, and ask her to whisper the name of the card she is thinking of. The sudden intimacy is strange, and it ramps up some tension.

'Four of Hearts,' she whispers, as if you've just asked for her PIN.

You'll have to take her word for it. Now give it a beat, as if you are doing something with that information. Let your focus pass through her and tense the muscles in one hand and then the other. Act like she wasn't supposed to notice anything. Then let go, sit back – very far away from the glass now – and ask her to find the Four of Hearts and remove it. 'It should be different,' you say, with uncertainty.

She looks through the cards in her hand but is unable to find the Four of Hearts.

You have shifted your breathing to your chest and sound a little nervous. 'Not there at all?' Laugh, like a great trick has just happened by accident. 'There you go! Amazing!'

'Where is it?' she asks, uncertain if this was the plan.

Respond by looking around on the table. She should do the same. Allow her to find it under the glass – it will be face down – and express enormous surprise and delight that that could be it.

When it turns out to be her card, enjoy the miracle with her. Then, mumbling something like 'Well it won't get any better than that', retrieve your cards and take your leave, a note of bafflement still signalling the fortuitous impossibility of the whole thing. Gather them up and go, because any other conversation will now be awkward. (You're a *magician*. What are you going to do, talk to her or let her buy you a drink?)

The trick is done, and now hopefully the deeper magic will happen as she tries to recreate the story for herself. It will be hard for her to join up the dots any other way than you have left them arranged, in the dappled light of her memory. What is her story?

Picking the card will be murky. She was embarrassed at her own shuffling and wasn't paying too much attention immediately after that. Later on, you asked her to whisper the name of the card *you are thinking of* for a reason – as opposed to *the card you picked*. Some people will confuse events and remember they merely thought of one at the start. Especially when they are recounting the trick to a friend and wanting to make it sound as impressive as possible (this is not a conscious manoeuvre: I have done it myself many times and fooled myself without realizing). If they do misremember the start of the story as *I shuffled the cards and thought of one*, then they have greatly increased the miracle.

From whatever half-memory remains of how the Four of Hearts was chosen, the story skips to when you said it would start – which is after the card is already secretly under the glass, and the others smeared across the table. And here's something that's easy to remember: *you never touched the cards.* You were so fair about that. She can remember your hands on hers and thinking about whether you could touch any of the cards if you wanted to. But you didn't. So you never touched the cards, that was clear. She thought of a card (or maybe she picked one), she shuffled them, you never touched them, maybe she even spread them out (she collected them up, so that would be easy to misremember too).

If you are a close-up conjuror with a restaurant residency, this trick will inevitably be interrupted by a waiter, and usually just after the card has vanished from between her hands. Your heart will plummet at the timing of the interruption, and you may succumb to a panicky kind of nausea as he reaches to remove the glass from the table. Such are the perils of working as a restaurant magician: you're one step up from a rose seller, as a friend put it. But before you can work out how best to continue, a beautiful thing will happen: he will lift the glass and the card will travel with it, stuck to the bottom with condensation. Your lady will miss this fact, not even registering the waiter, as she is too busy looking for the very same card. He, however, noticing the card stuck to the underside, will remove it, sheepishly sensing he may have interrupted a card game or trick, and offer it to her, with the words that you will never forget: 'Sorry, was this your card?' And this woman's trick now becomes: *the magician made my card disappear and then a second later the waiter brought it over from the other side of the room.* And you were right: it won't get any better than that.

The process of separate world-building, begun with an encounter, a question, has been sustained and calcified by a story. False memory and confirmation bias will be affected by her emotional response to the experience, so it's important it was positive (does she wish to embellish it because it was fun or reject it because the magician was creepy?). And so the conjuror has a peculiar perspective on how we form stories and fool ourselves, and then try to fool others. The story of the *amazing* holiday, the story of riots and election fraud. Most of all romantic relationships, which when ended we reduce to a simple story – *he was a nightmare, she was sweet but just impossible* – which spares us further heartbreak but does not come close to a messy truth. We tell these stories, and after a while they feel familiar enough to be reality. Perhaps we don't say what we believe as much as we come to believe what we say.

The end of the world

Such stories might grow to have extraordinary power in our inner lives, and we will often battle to keep them coherent if reality forces us to face incompatible facts. A famous example of the stressful feeling of dissonance that tends to occur is cited in the literature: the strange story of The Seekers. This small Chicago-based UFO religion predicted that the world would end with a huge flood at 7 a.m. on 21 December 1954. The believers *really* believed it. They quit their jobs, left their families, and gave away their money and possessions. They were entirely convinced they would leave the soon-to-be-deluged Earth aboard a flying saucer on the fateful morning.

The shy group reluctantly attracted some publicity, and among those whose interest was aroused was a trio of social psychologists: Leon Festinger, Henry Riecken and Stanley Schachter. They managed to infiltrate the group in order to observe the goings-on at close quarters. Once initiated, they watched as the group was informed twice – presumably by prank calls – that the saucer would arrive early, each time failing to do so. But their morale persisted.

The story of the approaching hour is bizarre and touching. At midnight before the Apocalypse, the group is expecting to be visited by an alien who will escort them to the craft. They have already removed all metal items, including fly zips and bra straps, following instructions received by the group leader in the normal way: via automatic writing performed while in psychic communication with the planet Clarion. Midnight blankly passes, after a succession of clocks have been consulted with increasing desperation. These few minutes of painful hope and confusion must have been excruciating for the scientists present. The alien visitor fails to appear, and for four further hours the group sits in silent incredulity. The end of the world, for which they left their families and gave away a lifetime of belongings, has not happened. There are tears and disbelief. Then, at 4.45 a.m., a message comes from Clarion in the same way as before, via the hand of the now very emotional leader. But this time the dispatch brings ground-breaking news: the group has spread so much love that God has chosen to spare the planet. In a happy volte-face they have saved the world through their unwavering belief.

After this comes an outpouring of evangelism. In a direct reversal of their former stance the invigorated group now fervently seeks publicity to promote their cosmic message. The curious story concludes with The Seekers Christmas-carolling in the neighbourhood and being attacked by two hundred exasperated locals.

Strictly speaking, the participation of the observers in the events they are supposed to be observing and the role of a story-hungry media do rather contaminate the study and make it hard to draw accurate or objective conclusions. Furthermore, the investigators *predicted* the result for which they hoped, namely that the group would strengthen their message following the failure of reality to concur, which suggests they had an interest in telling the story that confirmed their own prediction; to have their prophecy fail would clearly involve its *own* dissonance. Thus there are sound reasons to reserve scepticism regarding some of their conclusions, but hey, it's a good story. And it's nice to tell it, regardless of the facts.

The group's dissonance, and the scientists', and now perhaps ours. Compelling stories and awkward reality come into collision, and the response from all of us is not to undo the belief, but to ramp up the message. Thus, when we try to convince someone that her beliefs are false by presenting the contradicting facts of reality, it has the curious effect of only strengthening what was already there.

On this note of dissonance . . . in my show *Infamous* I performed my version of mediumship. After ditching a card trick from the show early in the run, my co-collaborators Andy Nyman and Andrew O'Connor, along with your author, needed to find another use for the expensive bank of fifty-two chairs which formed part of the set but now had no good reason to be there. In the routine we devised and tried out the same night, I invited members of the audience on to the stage and offered them messages from their deceased friends and relatives. I was able to pass on familiar types of proof – names and details I could not have known, and which could not be explained by the usual cold-reading. However, unusually for this type of demonstration, I peppered the readings with reminders that I was lying, that I had no psychic ability, and that the spirits were telling me nothing, even as they were apprising me of the most strikingly specific information. The result, we felt, was effective, and certainly uncomfortable and emotional. It was not unusual for the people involved to weep, and then a second later, baffled at the deception of which they were being reminded, to laugh. It occupied an interesting space theatrically, playing as it did in the sort of dissonance I've described, and remains one of my favourite pieces I've performed.

One night, after the show, I left the theatre through the stage door where a few people had gathered. One of them, a girl, waited for the others to leave and then asked me if I might put her in touch with her grandmother, who had recently passed away. I was surprised that she had concluded that I could genuinely speak with the dead, so I replied, 'Oh God, I'm so sorry – I hope it was clear from the show that none of that is real.'

'Oh yes,' she replied, 'I know it's not real, but would you still be able to put me in touch with my grandmother?'

It was, to me, an affecting aspect of the kind of cognitive juggling Festinger and his colleagues had written about, and points to why I find it hard to laugh at the waiting group of zipless Seekers. According to his theory, when we have to hold two inconsistent ideas simultaneously, we change them until they can be brought into line. We experience the discomfort, or dissonance, and tend to either rationalize or edit out what cannot be made to agree. Somehow this girl was able to hold comfortably in balance both ideas – the compelling desire for connection, along with the knowledge that no such connection was possible – perhaps by shifting one or the other to form a vague rationale of *well, whatever he calls it, I'd really like him to do it.* Furthermore, it was clear that the emotional story had trumped the rational one: the illusion proved more compelling than the assurances that it was really just that.

If magic, then, contains any secret worth discovering, it is that we are master editors of our experience, and live out an irresistible urge to form stories from the data we are offered – stories by which we then come to live. The ability to form a fiction and stick to it presumably served our ancestors, as communities were then and are now bound together by shared stories. When a nation participates in one, it can be led to war, and we can enjoy a powerful tribal identity. Perhaps an echo of this is our love of fiction, which tickles the same part of our brain. Films and novels seem to grip us because we can experience the thrill of danger and extremity of situations without having to suffer ourselves. Our motor neurons fire up in sympathy with a hero's plight and whisk us away on a parallel emotional ride, permitting us to vent our aggressive, anti-social feelings at no personal risk.

Magic tricks rarely involve convincing personal danger, but they are still built around the notion of plight, of overcoming the odds.* They are spun from a moment of eye contact, where we meet one another as a set of needs to be answered. And stories, or at least the ones we care about, are always, deep down, about suffering.

---

* I've watched more than my fair share of escapologists during my career, and I think the only time I truly cared about the jeopardy constructed around the escape was in an episode of the Amazon Prime series *Nathan For You*, entitled 'The Claw of Shame'. Our hero risks becoming a sex offender, training for months to pull off an escape in which he has ninety seconds to escape from handcuffs before a robot arm pulls his pants down and exposes him to a group of young children. The mock solemnity of the whole event, the local police and officials duped into taking part, and the kids ultimately finding the whole thing hilarious, made for surely the best escape stunt ever staged.

THESE ARE THE PEOPLE
WHO POPULATE OUR LIVES

Shortly before departing this fleeting world for the Regions of Immortal Felicity, we may be accorded a fresh perspective on the life we have lived. We can try to guess what insight this final vantage point will offer us, but even if we could foresee it with accuracy, it's unclear how thoroughly we should incorporate such grave last-moment wisdom into our lives while we are still robust and thriving.

Take the injunction 'Live each day as if it were your last'. Certain scenarios race through my mind. Is this an enjoinder to spend each day in bed, high on morphine, groaning and soiling the sheets? If not, then presumably it is an imperative to complete a bucket-list of tickable pursuits: to travel and bungee-jump and meet the great and good. But if ample time stretches ahead of me, what when that list is complete? Must I then draw up a B-list, and so on? It seems like an exhausting prospect that would only make me unbearable to be around. And I am unsure that such dramatic adventures would be my choice of activity on my final day of existence. I think instead I'd like to write something about it all, have some friends over, and then curl up with my partner. The sourdough bread from the café round the corner would feature somewhere. Whatever it would be, clearly a life that is about to be extinguished suggests different priorities from one which we hope will flicker and blaze for some time to come.

Perhaps, instead, the glib edict is badly articulating the benefits of mindful gratitude. A few weeks ago, Doodle, my recalcitrant beagle-basset who has never shown any interest in cuddling, affection or even eye contact, climbed up on to the sofa next to me as I worked on this book. I felt a warm shiver as time decelerated, and I paid complete attention to the unfolding of this entirely new development. The cross of two disinterested and wilful breeds, she has never warmed to physical proximity, and appears, whenever picked up, to be counting in her head until she is put back down. Now here she was, pitching her porcine frame up and on to the soft green cushion, climbing inelegantly atop me, one front paw on my laptop, another on my testicles, bearing down with the surprising heft of her barrel-chested frame. In this position she waited, motionless, head turned to the side to avoid meeting my gaze, and I realized this was not, in the strictest sense, affection. She was interested in moving *through* me to occupy what her radar had identified as the warmest spot in the room, beneath her inconvenient master. When I failed to move or simply dematerialize, she contained her disappointment and took the next best seat – next to me, huddled close. She curled herself around and squeezed into the trough of pillow alongside my right leg, closed her eyes, and was snoring sonorously within a few seconds. Aware this arrangement would be unlikely to happen again for some time, I stopped typing and looked down at her and our little scene with a warm glow of gratitude. *Here's me and there's my dog sleeping next to me. This is perfect.* Perhaps this is the kind of mindfulness truly intended by the instruction to treat each day as if it were your last.

I became conscious of that moment and savoured it. I stored the image somewhere in the cloisters of my imagination for later recall. But as I think back now I realize how badly I did so – I cannot remember which way she faced, for example – and the mental snapshot is grainy. I am recreating it like a police illustrator sketching a face from a few details given by a crime victim. Nothing is quite how it was. And even though the perspective committed to memory may be first-person (looking down at my chest, stomach and legs, the dog to my side), the resulting memory feels strangely third-person. We save these moments but when we retrieve them we are handed something fabricated and vague, an artist's impression. How immortal the present seems as we ride it out, and how hard it will be to find it again with precision.

Which takes us to another edict, 'Live in the present moment', which can also miss the mark, as generally we are occupied in projects that, like it or not, must take place over a span of time. It is true that we become too easily fixated on what-is-yet-to-be at the expense of being properly present in the world, and get stuck in reliving patterns imprinted long ago in the past. We are well advised to lean a little more into the present, and above all to *notice* more. Not only to pay closer attention to what lies before us in the world, but also to improve an inward attention towards the recurring and familiar restrictions we impose upon ourselves as we dodge opportunities for growth. But it is still the case that our present moments take place before a contingent future, and to deny the relevance of that future is to conjure a strangely anaemic version of the world. Moreover, to free ourselves up to an honest relationship with the present moment, there is much in our past we can learn to accommodate on more friendly terms. It is surely the ambiguous interplay and relationship *between* the past, present and future that we should be encouraged to better understand and embrace. In our age, as our sources of learning are reduced to a too-comfortably-curated social media feed, the lessons of history are slipping through our scrolling fingers. And to abandon all care as to what lies ahead may be to exist in a state of depression: to live without desire. Part of our task is to place ourselves correctly in time, not to deny it. Only its passage permits change and purpose: meaning requires a story, which occurs across time.

Rather than concern ourselves with those edicts to live within the confines of one slippery instant or another, I'd like to suggest a different thought to carry with us: a pre-emptive gleaning of advice from our future selves. It seems to me that at some point we are almost certain to look back on our lives and consider in an uncommon light the familiar *people* who appeared there. I suspect we will look back over the arbitrary stretch of time which turned out to be ours and consider the array of characters that filled it. We might imagine them now like the company of a play lining up for the curtain-call. Some played principal parts, many more were cast in minor or supporting roles. Most of them were identifiable sources of pleasure or pain in our lives.

Some years ago, for example, I worked alongside someone who often annoyed me, but to whom I felt loyal. Finding myself irritated following a phone call with him one morning over breakfast, I applied something like a Stoic move to ease the annoyance: *He is doing his best, given whatever circumstances he finds himself in. He is not on this earth to make my life easier. Does it matter that he might seem a bit inept in some areas?* These words helped, and gave way to a further thought: *He's been with me a while; he's part of my gang.* Then – *Oh, I have a gang! These are the people who surround me.* My mind flitted to two or three other people who had been bothering me of late. They too were part of the troupe of people and colleagues I saw frequently. From a perspective of imagined hindsight, I viewed them all from the end of my life. Those who had irked me now appeared differently, triggering a new fondness. They were the ones I had been apportioned to fill my world and time, the people I knew. They were the people who had populated my life.

To glean something worthwhile from this unashamedly

self-centred perspective, let's take less interest in those people we unambiguously like. They already have our appreciation. In the same way that our pain-free times of physical comfort tend to slip by unnoticed, and we only really register the disturbance of an ache or irritant as it makes itself known, let it be the more conspicuous figures – therefore predominantly the painful or the powerful ones – that concern us for the moment.

Here then, ready for their bow, are our parents, who loved us in their imperfect way and whom we loved back in ours; who shaped us more than anyone; who instilled in us clusters of energized sensitivity towards certain triggers that would come to shape the emotional landscape of our adult world; and who died before we could say everything we should. Most parents want us to say *thank you*, while most children hope for *sorry*. But now all tensions are put aside and they step forward to acknowledge our applause.

Next to them we find our romantic partners, who despite all hopes caused us turmoil and pain; upon whom we unintentionally inflicted indelible suffering; who loved us and disappointed us and made us disappointed in ourselves as we loved them. With the hindsight of our final days, we see that if they had a task, it was to point us towards the difficult formative work of growing and being more alive in this life, because without them we would have stagnated into insufferable, unchecked versions of ourselves. We remember the break-ups that brought turbulence and tragedy. Several times our world fell apart. Now, as we consider these people who occupied such vital territory, comes the clarity of that repeated thought: *Oh, these were the people who populated my life. The people who, at different times, were there with me, making me who I became. These are those people.*

While those we loved most might take first bow, let's arrange the remaining cast for their call. Next to step up are those with whom we worked and who filled our days; those who made us laugh and those who drove us mad; those we would have loved to remove from our lives completely. The people who worked with us but seemed constitutionally unable to do their jobs correctly. Various acquaintances we loathed whose calls we would leave to ring out, the phone dying in spasms on the desk like a fish flapping out of water. The neighbour whom we would cross the road or duck into shops to avoid. Those people to whom we grew accustomed but derided behind their backs. Members of the ensemble that stung us regularly with one of a million tiny arrows. And, further on, the supporting cast of familiar cab drivers and local shop attendants – people towards whom we harboured no marked feelings, but who formed a vital stratum of recognizable reference points, a bedrock of easy contours that helped define our days. They too smile and step forward to bob and curtsey, and as we catch ourselves sighing with a new-found affection, we realize: *Ah, these too were the people who populated my life.*

Now we are surprised to see those people we knew of only from a distance, but whose presence nonetheless shaped some part of our soul. Here is the actor we admired and with whom we grew improperly obsessed; the writer or singer who gripped our imagination for decades; the luminary upon whom we modelled ourselves and with whom we once fantasized sharing a great friendship. There, the one or two cherished celebrities we did briefly meet, but then only showcased our proclivity for the searingly idiotic turn of phrase – encounters we have replayed in the heat of anguished nights ever since. Behind these respected names, a discomfited figure steps forward meekly: a treasured porn-star for whom we spent a notable chunk of our life trawling through backwaters of the Internet with an indecorous resolve. These characters too, who intimidated or obsessed us, are now revealed as vital roles that contributed to our particular story.

That was our time, and those were the people who shared it with us. Those who loomed too large are thus reduced in stature and shrunk to life-size. The people we loathed or feared, such as those who pummelled us in our sleeping bag far from home, are lifted into the light and forgiven their sins. A fondness creeps in and pettiness dissolves. These people, even those we despised, are the ones *we* met, *we* knew and *we* thought about. They were *our* personal share of humanity, our largely local consortium of aggressors and supporters, each of which were doing their best at life within their limited means, as did we. Unlike theatrical characters of course, they exist beyond what we saw of them. But they were *our* network, curated by taste and chance; they constituted *our* matrix of relationships in which we would come to show ourselves, for better or worse. Some of them seemed to have a power over us, yet as their power now seems diminished, we see that the generous benefactor who bestowed such mighty capability was *us*; it was *we* who granted it to them. We were their co-star, director and audience. We did much to reduce them, enlarge them, control them, recreate them in our image. In truth they were fellow inhabitants of Earth, complex and struggling like us, finding their way, clashing with the world in their own manner, wanting to be loved, letting people down, translating their fears into a thousand strange behaviours. And they were the ones given to us as company.

A further point. Normally, as applauded actors leave the stage, we might be stirred to consider what the play has left us with. They have played their parts, said their lines, and left us with some kernel of meaning. What, now, are we to take from their work? What remains? What message, about life, or about ourselves? Only by reviewing the dramas that we shared with this particular set of people, with the distance that comes from hindsight, will we find any answers to these important questions. Our self has meaning only by extending out through relationships with others, and thus it is by reflecting on our interpersonal history that we will truly see ourselves. The clues as to what it all meant, all we have learned, all that we became, are offered within those ties and affiliations, and can be found scattered there. By contrast, our mere *intentions* of goodness, and private thoughts of love that fell stillborn before the world of people, amounted to nothing. Our true nature resided in the specific day-to-day content and tone of our daily interactions with these people, to whom we were largely paying scant attention.

Irrespective of how we like to see ourselves, the truth of the picture is contained across a thousand recollections of our words and actions stored in the memories of waiters and colleagues and lovers. That is our legacy, which, when we are gone, will be found in these people: the afterglow that follows us.

These are the people who populate our lives.

VIRUS

I am sat wedged along the length of a tiny sofa, slippered feet pushing against the far arm. My laptop is supported wonkily on my outstretched legs by a cushion bearing the embroidered features of a vigilant beagle, for which we had to settle, as a beagle-basset-cross is hard to find off the shelf. This dwarf settee is the principal resting place offered by a cabin I keep, away from London as a clifftop retreat. My partner and I are here along with said hybrid (Doodle), and our Tibetan terrier (Humbug). A mucky stove fire is slowly toasting the first, who snores and twitches before it, dreaming of the bunny rabbits she only encounters in the country. Other than the questionable five dog beds, there is a kettle, a place to drink coffee and look at the sea, a whimsical relationship with WiFi, and a copper bath which on a good day takes thirty minutes to fill.

Forty-three miles away, my father is dying in his bedroom.

I cannot visit him, nor my mother, who says she is looking in every half an hour to study his chest for signs of movement. We are unable to be together because of government-enforced restrictions following the COVID-19 outbreak which is most likely responsible for his sudden decline – an unexpected catalyst for an already dire tally of ailments and terrors. So I am secluded in this cabin, a model of isolation, with only the possibility of FaceTime to offer faint support to Mum or convey a juddery goodbye to Dad. And we are told that any funeral will be only for her, my brother and me to attend, and we would have to remain two metres from each other. Such was today.

WEDNESDAY

Mum, when asking the palliative nurses how she might best give her unconscious husband food and water, was told not to bother. It would serve no purpose and only risk him choking. That is a strange thing: amid so many invisible forces which are slowly removing him from us, his wife, who has nurtured him through years of deterioration, must now *guarantee* complete and rapid demise with such an obscene omission of care. *Don't feed him* . . . and now perhaps you will always feel the tiniest bit complicit in his death.

A side-note: I have been asked to be a down-the-line guest on a radio show which the BBC are continuing to air to uplift its isolated listeners. I messaged to say I should bow out, as all told I don't think I can offer quite the pep and brio that comprise my brief. Perhaps that was wrong, as many people will be going through similar ugliness. But for now I am loath to disclose publicly what is happening. My phone is already a little too jumpy with entreaties from people I don't know well as to how I am faring in lockdown, and I'm not eager to encourage further cause for commiseration. I feel a sense – and I am also aware of this when talking to people who have had a cancer diagnosis conferred upon themselves or their loved ones – of needing to control the edges of a narrative. Responses of cloying sympathy, horror, misjudged comparisons or alternative health advice are not welcome.

I mentioned that I had declined this interview, via Twitter, to a friend who is a vicar. In return he offered to privately pray for my father. In the past, I have had Christian friends volunteer to do the same when they believed I needed it, and each time I felt oddly violated. There is often an aura of smug appropriation to the offer which hijacks the story one is being careful to manage and opens it up to a different authorship. Suddenly, someone seems poised to take credit for any hint of improvement, to interpose themselves into a private wordless space and introduce their own language. The idea has always made me bristle. This time I feel differently. Not because I imagine that the professional prayers of a friendly parson might improve Dad's situation any more than the petitions of the laity: he is already being kept adrift upon a one-way stream of morphine, which has now quieted the groaning and discomfiture that punctuated my earlier video calls with Mum. This time I am moved by the kindness of the gesture.

It reminds me of a sight that has stayed with me since the funeral of my uncle a few years ago. I was travelling within the languid cavalcade of motors to a chapel in Chislehurst, that great homeland of ageing aunts and their ailing husbands, staring through the window at the busy shoppers and pedestrians, watching them notice us. Then, among them on a side-hill, a distant dark-dressed man stopped, removed his cap and bowed his head, standing unstirring in a moving gesture of respect I had not encountered before. That silent display cut through the everyday bustle which so strangely continues around death. How odd it seems that others are not sharing in our grief, how foreign that backdrop of teeming indifference. This man offered a signal that was not merely a reverence for the dead, but effectively a solidarity with the living: a recognition that our worlds had changed, that the air between us had been altered, and that a single exhibition of unanimity from the far side of the high street could honour the strange, slow universe that now wrapped around us.

This friend's offer to pray for my father feels like a similar acknowledgement. My family's new, acute, slo-mo relationship to the world, so intensely private and *here*, will also be quietly reflected *there*, in his church or at his bedside or wherever a thoughtful parish priest makes his appeals.

There is a horror and worry and fascination around the thought of an impending death that I find makes me unusually present, and prone to a kind of prickly sense-heightening in which every detail and sound is lifted and made available before me – *these are the crows who call and caw while my father is dying; this is the silver-black evening sea which roars while my father is dying.* I feel in complete attendance upon every sensation, every moment. This is, I suppose, anxiety, but I am also calm. *Apprehension* is an appropriate word, with its twin meanings of 'unease' and 'awareness'. I feel unusually conscious (I suppose

I am remaining prepared for the call that says he has gone); I am apprehending. The word also suggests confinement, as in the apprehension of a perpetrator: there is a sense of a very private prison in which all this is housed, a separation of me-with-all-this-inside from the outside world of things.

But with the offer of prayer, so alien to my irreligious disposition, these incarcerated sensations now slide from my insides, through the slither of salty air that immediately surrounds my skin, to find a sympathetic echo many miles away, without demand or disturbance, in the pastoral contemplation of another soul and a moment of muttered supplication sent out into the same night.

THURSDAY

While yesterday I typed the paragraphs above, I did not know that my father was taking, or maybe giving, his last breath. Mum, passing his room as the medics in her front garden donned the protective masks and aprons *du jour*, noticed that a new silence had settled thickly into the house. COVID-19 had burrowed its ashen fingertips into a Bromley bungalow and taken him from us.

In a gesture of unexpected kindness, it spared my father a

long decline from blossoming bone cancer. He had been unaware of both the worldwide plague and the personal one: both had arrived during a long hospital stay and he had caught wind of neither.

It turned out that his last waking act, several days before, had been to watch John Wayne, in bed, on the portable DVD player I'd bought him. It was only a week since the doctor had called for his elaborate agglomeration of daily medications to cease, which had resulted in him quite suddenly feeling the best he had for years. He was kissed by my mother as he told her how much he had enjoyed the film (we used to make fun of his movie choices but I shall watch this one, to see what final thoughts played in his head as he drifted off), and then he fell asleep. If he discerned anything over the stretch of dark time that followed, he might have wondered at the sudden change for the worse. It stings me that he may have questioned the minimal contact from Mum, and that he would have remained alone during his last hours, hand unheld, firmly denied the presence of a (scattered and isolating) family by his side.

Sat here by the sea yesterday afternoon, out in the light and breeze, I suddenly felt the vibration of my silenced phone against my thigh. Three or so murmurs and I knew this was the news; knew as I reached for it, before I saw the picture of Mary Berry illuminate my screen (I use bad lookalikes as contact pictures on my phone, and Mum begrudgingly announces herself with the exacting features of the nation's favourite pâtissier). I answered, alert to whatever tone in Mum's voice was to follow, attentive to the moment, clear that Dad had died and this was to be the instant I found out.

'Did you get my text?' Her words were disorienting.

'No . . .'

'Dad died about half past one.'

'What time is it now?' (Why did the time suddenly matter?)

'Nearly three.'

I asked what had happened, and she explained about the medics and the silence and how they had attributed his death to COVID. The doctor had remotely observed him before he died via the jagged resolution of her iPhone camera and declared him most likely in its grip. Now he would be one of the statistics of the hour, part of that growing morbid tally about which the rest of us shake our heads while we learn to bake. Whenever I hear those numbers, I think of pyramid schemes, which we are told can never work because within ten levels of three friends selling to three friends each, there would be no one left in the country to participate. And here it is, progressing along the same path.

A death in the family has turned out to be a series of disappointing slips. Mum texts me the news, I miss the text because I'm writing about him dying, and I don't hear of the event for an hour and a half. My brother had FaceTimed Dad the day before, and spoken to him; Dad had feebly responded, opening an eye, maybe both, for a moment. I had not thought to communicate in this way until my brother told me about it, and even then I still did not do so. It felt a strange way to tell him I loved him, to say thank you, with Mum holding her pink diamanté-cased iPhone 6 near his blurry, grizzled face, my own features rendered in miniature in the bottom corner, watching myself in that stupid way we do – *this is what you look like saying farewell to your dying father*. And part of me wonders: what if he didn't know he was dying? Would he really want his family offering emotional goodbyes? It would hardly be encouraging. So I didn't speak to him, which now sits uncomfortably. Instead I suppose I have fonder, three-dimensional, life-size memories from our last time together: visiting him in hospital after rehearsals for *Showman*, with a rucksack of cheese, crackers and pickled onions, encouraging him to eat; he insisting I take back that DVD player I had initially bought for him to use in the hospital, as the nurses couldn't be trusted. (It turned out that twenty years before and in a different hospital he had once caught an Angel of Mercy rifling through his locker. Distrust had lingered.)

So, a series of second-rate omissions and botches: I did not say goodbye, I did not hold his hand, I missed the text. After talking to Mum, my partner and I fortified ourselves with nachos and he drove me to hers. My brother travelled over to join us, and he and I sat on the back patio with her, the regulated distance from each other. Mum had been instructed to fully self-isolate for two weeks. We could neither touch her nor enter the house. Dad had been removed: a few hours before, a team in hazmat suits had arrived and extracted him like a piece of radioactive material. As we talked into the dark, another comic incongruity: between us, on the garden table for the taking should we want them, Dad's wedding ring and a nine-pack of Andrex Classic Clean.

Mum was exhausted. Ronnie the golden lab gave up petitioning us for affection and took fourth position on the grass. My brother thought we shouldn't stroke him in case he might later carry infection between us and Mum. We had arrived around sunset, in thick coats and hats, so the cold and the black of the spring night came soon. But as it approached, in the stillness of the blue-grey twilight, we were surprised by the evening star, unusually bright, seemingly alone. It was puncturing the cloudless hour in a watchful, gleaming glint of brilliance. Or was it, my brother wondered, a satellite? A plane? Privately imagining it was Dad but not wanting to say so, we each took turns, beneath his paternal gaze, to urinate behind a tree.

When we left, I took the ring and left the toilet paper.

FRIDAY

We are not going to have a funeral. Instead of the three of us travelling separately to an allocated room and sitting apart without a service of any note, we will get his ashes sent to the house. This irreligious approach is common now, we are assured. It feels odd, though. Another point of emptiness in a very empty scenario. Later in the year, or next year, we'll have a memorial get-together. We'll think of somewhere to bestrew his mortal cinders. Already we are considering revenge-scatterings around the school swimming pool where he was an instructor for many years, and which has lain dormant and drained since he retired. Until then, while Mum quarantines for two weeks, there will have to be a container (an actual urn?) sitting glaringly around her house like a guest who won't leave the party.

The oddness of this virus-hour – emails contain a hundred variations on the phrase 'these strange times' – cloaks loss with an unexpected tranquillity. His individual death, from one perspective, is made insignificant by the numbers, one near-infinitesimal point among statistics I don't know how to compare to anything. My father is now contained within that sombre register, and rather than feel he has vanished point-lessly within it, there is a strange sort of peace that comes with the knowledge. Commonly we might feel a sense of absurdity when we lose a loved one. I remember a friend's friend who was killed out on his bicycle when his dog, trotting alongside on the lead, crossed in front and caused the bike to forward-flip and the rider to smash down head-first. In Dad's case, though, death's preposterousness has been mitigated by what feels like shared consternation and understanding across the world. It makes more sense, now that a blanket absurdity has been unfurled across the globe.

An event related to this feeling of shared surreality: after seeing Mum on Wednesday, my partner and I drove home to nearby London to diligently lock ourselves away. Thursday morning – yesterday – I went to the local Sainsbury's to gather supplies for the next stretch of isolation. As I picked up a hand of bananas and wondered how many others had touched it before me, a flustered security guard came over and told me to leave the basket and exit the shop. His accent was thick and panicked and it was hard to understand. 'Leave my shopping here and go? OK . . .' I did as I was told, wondering at the nature of this invisible emergency. As I stepped outside, I could see across the road a pack of builders yelling and pointing, urging the traffic and me to get out of the way. Perhaps something was about to explode. I walked away, in the direction they were gesticulating, and as I turned back to look, *Sainsbury's was on fire.*

And a *proper* fire. It was a small branch, but with a tower block extending above it which, I presumed, was home to self-isolating residents. One corner of the lower floor of the block (which coincided with the roof of the supermarket) was given over to a staggering mantle of black smoke surrounding a heart of orange flames, which alone spanned perhaps a dozen storeys. In my rush to get to safety, I barely had time to compose a photograph. Within ten seconds, three young locals, forgetting the distancing rules, assembled on the same corner and did the same. A Spanish-sounding girl who lived directly opposite fled her house, eccentrically using her phone to make an emergency call, perhaps unaware of the searing whoop and whine of engines that already saturated the air.

My instinct, as I WhatsApped the photo to my partner and headed towards a different grocery shop, was to vaguely attribute the fire to the virus. Perhaps it was an arson attack and an early sign of civil unrest. The same soft edges of disaster . . . *strange times*. A bizarre thought upon which to reflect, but sincerely felt in the moment. *Of course Sainsbury's is on fire. This is all a disaster movie.*

How sensitive we are to cinematic cliché when our days are tinged with apocalypse. The zombie genre (and that of the pandemic disaster) has unearthed every delicious possible way of showing an ailing world's efforts to hang on to normality and all its artificial trappings. The gaudy excesses of the media are a favourite: these films frequently offer scenes of news anchors struggling with due diligence while succumbing to infection or even attack. There is something affecting about the familiar faces of television being brought low. On my

Twitter feed, I watched the American talkshow host Seth Meyers introducing what I presume to be the only section of his show that they could still air, from a near-empty, strangely laughless studio. A week or so later he did the same from the landing of what looked like his home. I had been a guest on the same show a few months before, back when having guests in your studio was a thing. Watching them persevere impressively in this makeshift way was absolutely a swing to a cinematic reality. *Here Seth Meyers plays himself in a great scene where they can't make the show properly any more because of the virus.* The struggle of TV to preserve the facade of TV was captivating.

In the same way that dust and ten thousand fluttering papers now fill the air every time a building collapses on screen (two ingredients of real-life mise-en-scène that hadn't occurred to us pre-9/11), now themes of social distancing, mask-wearing and protecting the elderly will become the movie clichés in yet-to-be-made infection plots. Empty supermarket shelves are already a genre staple, associated with a level of violent looting far beyond the stockpiling of toilet paper and pasta (but not for some reason fusilli, which does on reflection seem a bit nineties, like Pinot Grigio and deep-pan pizza). If looting happens during COVID season then the movies have prepared us, and it will not be shocking. If hooded addicts wield guns behind the drug counter while you're trying to find an inhaler for your asthmatic son, you won't be entirely surprised. You'll adjust very quickly.

Of course the point of things feeling like a movie is that they are safe for us in the end. We can tickle our primal fight-or-flight response and know, as our ancient amygdala gets suckered, that we are in truth safe and secure as long as we anti-bac and chew our popcorn properly. The movie-likeness of this current reality makes it hard to emotionally calibrate, and, if we are young and healthy, might even render some of the Hollywood-scented drama shamefully appealing. Feeling safe (because we believe we are not in a high-risk group) while watching the crisis unfold is precisely the way horror cinema works.

This virus has both taken my father and also provided the gentlest exit for him. It has stranded my quarantined mother with forms and phone calls and FaceTime, but it also feels like the world is bowing its head from across the street. If your father is to die, let it be quietly while the world is in movie pandemonium and well versed in absurdity.

THURSDAY, 18 JUNE

First permitted hug with Mum. She has lost a little weight and the bungalow has grown slightly. The ugly apparatus of accessibility, which had given the bathroom the air of a remedial assault course, has been dismantled.

We discuss the odd feeling that Dad's death hasn't happened. With no contact, no crying and hugging, and no funeral to think about, there has been no emotional proof that it happened at all. A pile of post-mortem paperwork and procedure has provided some drudging evidence for Mum. His mere absence is no proof: he hadn't been at home for six weeks anyway. The latest long stint at the hospital had brought the prognosis of extended cancer that turned out to mean little. Perhaps above all we need other people to verify such an event. Without face-to-face commiserations and embraces, is it less of a deal? Perhaps this is why I find myself reluctant to tell people, to mention it in texts, and hold back unless someone asks directly. The few sympathetic responses I have received are evidence that it has definitely happened, in fact the *only* evidence in the air. Otherwise, the tragedy has been softened and proliferated across a beleaguered and sympathetic globe, and in our curious isolation we are not − or certainly I am not – being made to confront anything in particular. It has happened, elsewhere, according to reports.

Another odd moment of letdown: as there was no funeral, Dad's ashes were sent to Mum's house, in a clear plastic bag. 'I've got Robert Brown for you,' the delivery person announced at her doorstep. Urns, it seems, do not come as standard; our choice, all considered, not to have a funeral qualified us for the cheapest possible container option. And aside from his wedding ring, I have asked to keep his aftershave. He used the same cheap brand all through my life. I shall smell it, frugally, as a means of recharging his memory – the splosh of him washing his razor in foamy black-peppered water in the sink, him wearing red shorts and a thin white T-shirt with a plump crescent of hairy belly disclosed between the two – should the details ever start to blur.

As I read back through these diary entries, I am struck by the fact that the story I am assembling for myself about Dad's death – a peaceful passing, and an unexpected sparing of pain – has about it that tidiness which does not measure up to the day-by-day blows of what happened in reality. I have already started to forget the bumpy confusion of it all, of my own emotional travels of these last months. The easy grace of the narrative has worked its way into my selective memory, quietly highlighting some parts and dropping others into shadow. Dad's death has become for me a story of how we form stories.

Earlier today I took my jacket to my local tailor's to fix its dangling sleeves, and the sight of Joe and Orhan back at work, roles resumed after whatever experiences had befallen them these last months, was glorious. The fact we had shared in the pandemic was somehow beautiful. We knew that we had each been through a similar journey: the shock of the cinematic mode of the world, perhaps the experience of loss, work concerns, astonishment at the sudden aliveness of being human, even amid disconnection and death. The very things which isolated us had brought us together – we had brushed shoulders with the Sublime.

We, customer and assistant, had separated, drunk deeply of compassion and mortality, and now would resume our most mundane relationships with each other. We knew the drill: in the shop we gawped at it all, enquired how it had been for each other, and said nothing of substance, already having reduced the plague to a topic of polite chatter – *strange times* – even while it still holds us in its grip. Underneath, I wanted to hug them both and thank them for reappearing; for managing the difficulty of months without work; for being among the people who populated my life, performing a service which had never moved me until now. Whatever they felt, we will have all forgotten this fresh glimpse of each other when I return to pick up the jacket, by which time we will have resumed our old places in a new world. But although I have lost something, I found something else in that shop: a memory of the world at a moment I can recall – like a painting restored to its original vibrancy, an age of obscuring dust and grime having been removed.

Meanwhile, that world is waking up after its enforced isolation, gingerly blundering out of bed, peering through the curtains, seeing what's outside. Which turns out to be shops reopening and our first handshakes in months. Supermarket shelves are stocked again. There is resigned talk of a second wave, so this dawn may be short-lived, but for now we are blessed: Aurora is welcoming us into the dayspring with masks and hand gel.

THE THINGNESS OF THINGS AND
A WONDER BEFORE THE WORLD

There's a saying among conjurors that magic transports us back to a childhood state of astonishment. Paul Harris, an American magician and writer hugely admired in the fraternity, describes a process whereby a baby arrives into the world full of wonder at everything, and embarks upon a gradual process of disenchantment as, piece by piece, the world becomes familiar. One experience at a time, amazement slowly recedes. It's only occasionally as adults that we experience true astonishment. Magic, according to Paul, brings it back. And that makes it important.

It's a lovely, clear idea, and I found it appealing when I read it: I had been worried that what I was doing was fatuous. I wondered, though, if I was just grabbing at something that made my job feel important. Perhaps it wasn't the full story. What about the grown-up *intellectual* pleasures of being fooled by a good trick? Worse, a magician who performs with bad breath and offensive patter clearly isn't transporting his audience anywhere important. Magic is surely only as good, or as beneficial, as the particular performer makes it – or more correctly, as the spectators experience it. I'm sure that Paul would agree and was principally thinking about *good* magic, but the trouble with believing your 'art' has an inherent value is that it shifts the responsibility away from you as a performer to *make* it valuable.

Good theatrical magic, for all its puzzles and fun, is hard pushed to take us to a place of true wonder because it is far from fathomless. There are no real paradoxes, no sense that the horizon is retreating the closer you get. The vast majority of grown-ups know they're being fooled, and are taking part in a sort of game when they watch or participate. True, it can be presented in more portentous, pretentious form, but a heavy mantle of solemnity is rarely worn convincingly. This is not always a metaphor: it is not uncommon at magic conventions to catch a glimpse of dirty trainers under the grim black robes of pot-bellied Bizarrists.

If we can't rely on obtaining lasting wonder from the professional makers of marvels, where might we find it? Why should it even be valuable? The very word 'wonder' has an air of sentimental shtick about it. It suggests, unfortunately, mouldering in a sort of daze, or seems to celebrate ignorance, which is very much at odds with what we usually consider constructive. Perhaps, then, its opposite lies somewhere in our day-to-day *busyness*. A day has been a success, we tend to feel, when we have got a lot done. I'm writing this at the close of such a day during which I have transformed a long-neglected utility room into a model of military, antiseptic orderliness. But it's notable that I choose to apply a Protestant work ethic as proudly to my spare time as I do to my labour. Busyness is promoted everywhere: it is a handy form of distraction, a way of tethering ourselves to that outer circumference of life.

An obsession with busyness is certainly no friend to wonder, and might explain why the latter seems so scarce. *Doing* could more often give way to a certain kind of *Being*. The normal mode of life, in which we are barely aware of our surroundings unless something is amiss, might occasionally yield to a richer sense of presence in the world. If we only know the Doing-mode, our soul will groan, and its buried Shadow – Being – will ominously rumble. At the very least it will lament in the early hours of the morning, before our ego has had a chance to resume its work of arranging life into neatly packaged narratives. We lie in semi-wakefulness, accompanying dark imaginings down long and moonless pathways. Often these are the disquieting thoughts that have not been honoured in the light of consciousness and now demand our attention.

Our ego is a nervous, organizing tool, a comic, fussy character, fluffing pillows and straightening whatnots on the mantelpiece. As it delivers each feisty punch to the sofa cushions it betrays a stratum of buried conflicts; its orderly arranging of candlesticks and carriage-clock discloses a horror felt at a world that might fall into disarray. This same fearfulness leaks through when, in the face of bad news, we keep our cool but reflexively line up our cutlery or straighten the folds in our clothing. I notice that when we are writing our stage shows and some troublesome issue arises, my director has a habit of lifting his chin and quietly humming show-tunes. It's a lovely, nonchalant move to reinstate a feeling of power and the comfort of order. We are always looking to control and arrange what we can, and when the world offers chaos, we move our sights to what we can marshal at the micro-level.

How do we tidy and arrange? We put things in boxes, we display by classification, we group by type. Our friend *ambiguity*, the signifier of messy reality, is ruthlessly expunged in the name of order. Take today's labour. When you open the cupboards now in my utility room, will you see a violent turmoil of raggedy cloths, fly sprays and a benumbing agglomeration of floor detergents? Not any more. Will you search fruitlessly for spare hangers among hairy dust and spider-ghosts? No longer. Instead, an enviable array of this year's finest cleaning products is sedulously deployed in rank and file with a precision to match the opening ceremony of the 2008 Beijing Olympics. Descaling agents now form the first proud, advancing row in my cupboard, their black-on-yellow no-nonsense labels leaving no doubt as to what fixed category is at play. Next to them, creamy bathroom cleaners. All was well until I found myself standing, motionless, grasping a bottle of HG's Scale Away spray, specifically yet *ambiguously* concocted for removing bathroom limescale. It perfectly straddled these two categories with its mocking depiction of a bathroom sink, bisected improbably into two adjacent demi-sinks, one a paragon of sparkling cleanliness and the other of yellowing, calcified neglect. In which row to put it? Tenuous harmony had yielded to entropy: I was floored by nuance.

At the time I was unaware that the act of tidying might later serve as a straining metaphor for the organizing impulse of our egos. But now, as I reflect upon the new arrangement of soaps, tubs of Vanish and pink, wool-specific gloop, I am reminded of Roland Barthes' psychoanalytical dissection of these detergents and powders: '"Persil Whiteness", for instance, bases its prestige on the evidence of a result; it calls into play vanity, a social concern with appearances, by offering for comparison two objects, one of which is whiter than the other.' He then refers to a detergent famous in France at the time, advertised as *cleaning in depth*, which Barthes notes is 'to assume that linen is deep, which no one had previously thought, and this unquestionably results in exalting it, by establishing it as an object favourable to those obscure tendencies to enfold and caress which are found in every human body'. Those that produce foam suggest luxury, airy elevation, even spirituality: this is 'the art of having disguised the abrasive function of the detergent under the delicious image of a substance at once deep and airy which can govern the molecular order of the material without damaging it'.

I appreciated none of these subtle, rich ramifications as I lined the products up, arranging merely by labels, reducing to stark nouns.

Then there is a deeper, personal poetry to some of these

objects which is lost in the pursuit of neatness. I felt its pang when I placed a plastic bottle of Goddard's Long Term Silver Polish at the front of the line of metal-cleaners. It was the same polish my father used when I was young. I saw the tablecloth pulled back from our 1950s mock-Regency dining table – a staple of home life in Purley. Strewn over the blue-grey under-felt were overlapping double-pages from the house newspapers: *Daily Mail* or *Croydon Advertiser*. The 'silver' – mostly plate, I feel obliged to add – would be marshalled upon the newspaper with ecclesiastical respect. Candlesticks, serving dishes and even medals were laid out and made ready for the serious busi-ness of being polished by a father eager to pass on ritual knowledge to a delicate son. Through an arcane process involv-ing pink paste, blue cloths, and yellow ones that you had to keep clean for buffing, tan tarnish would vanish and gleaming swells of mirror-like metal would be made manifest. It was, I suppose, a rare point of connection between us. For him, the ceremonial polishing of never-to-be-used silver must have resonated with the strains of his childhood, his struggling, large family and limited symbols of status. For me, it was probably just the pret-tiness. But our two searchlights crossed over in the darkness and something was illuminated.

All this inseparable from the close breath of my father; his hairy forearms; his polishing technique of small circles driven by a stubby index finger; his gentle admonishments if I was applying too much; the pleasure of cleaning the smooth belly of a pot versus the niggling intricacy of handles, which would accumulate tiny reserves of tenacious pink among the dips and whorls of silver filigree.

The image of that oval dining table, which had been in the family for fifty years, then shifted and undid itself. It has just been donated to the British Heart Foundation, after it failed to attract interest on eBay. It is six months since my father died and Mum, eager to make a few changes around the house, has let it go. I imagined it sitting at the back of a dingy (but oddly large) charity shop, surrounded by its red- and gold-striped chairs, one of which would have held Dad at the right-hand end of the table, almost every night, for half a century. I thought of the bickering that prickled there; my horror at runner beans and a childhood of fussy eating; my brother, sweet, fluffy-haired and somehow always in his jumper; Dad's stock declarations about Mum's excellent bolognese, her lovely lemon meringue. All those years of asking to leave the table – to 'get down'. Somehow, despite best efforts, we never really became one of those families that relished sprawling, shared meals, where they pass serving bowls and talk over each other like in films.

At whatever young age that was, I felt far from him, daily aware of the great divide between us, and oblivious to his mode of articulating love. A ride to the shops, pocket money or a lift home from school didn't register as important, whereas a needless rebuke when I came downstairs to record a show on the VCR – 'If you break it you pay for it!' – cut deeply. Yet now, those frustrated and helpless dispatches from a foreign land amount to a portrait of a man who was doing his best. They comprised our unsettled relationship, which grew better as we got older, and, perhaps, as he became more vulnerable. We expended so much effort along a journey that never quite found its destination, its place to simply *be*, other than perhaps in the accommodating, fond here-and-now-ness of talking with someone whose mind is touched by the first stirrings of Alzheimer's. In Mum's house now – *Mum's house!* – Dad no longer lingers, following a windy seaside scattering amid the kite-surfers. I looked around the bungalow for a tangible tribute to his endeavours, some evidence of *a life lived*, constructed from a necessitous and undereducated start. The search results were returned: some contents of the wardrobe (many of which were in black bin-bags); a bed that needed someone to sleep in it to break its morbid spell. And perhaps *me*. I must be some kind of awkward tribute to him.

Now I wonder about objects and my own death, and how a world of things I have built around me will be scattered – a library of treasures blindly sold, these clothes I have worn and loved thrown out or driven to Save the Children. This unexpectedly cruel aspect of objects: despite how much time we give them, they will have the last laugh, making *us* the objects of *their* possession, bound up in a dense back-and-forth game of identity. And when we go, it'll be some innocuous object we leave behind that will carry the weight of a life lived and catch someone's throat – our Kindle still charging by the bed, maybe, bringing them to a stinging standstill.

A moment's presence with the Goddard's brought this back. I held on to the bottle, feeling my father sealed within it like a message. The objects of our lives are tethered to associations that to a greater or lesser degree flesh them out and make them fully personal. Some are direct, like those of the silver polish, others less so, like Barthes' speculations as to the psychological ramifications of soap powders and detergents. This aura of meaning is inseparable from the object itself as it exists in our world, and in as much as it amounts to a kind of dialogue between us and it – the observer and the observed, subject and object – it is impossible to consider one without allowing for the other. Can I think at all without somehow implying an outside world of objects? Certainly much of our busyness seems to involve their handling or consideration: buying them, moving them from here to there, tidying them, passing them on, disposing of them. Can I perceive objects without involving a vibrant personal complex that roots them in my memories, goals, prejudices? Does it make sense to say things exist without context, without a meaning that I or someone gives them? If outer and inner worlds cannot be so easily sundered, does it make sense to think of them as two fundamentally independent realms in the way we do?

Inner and outer

Our model of perception normally runs as follows: a coffee cup or bottle of Goddard's exists in the real world, and then impacts our sensory system in such a way that our brain supplies us with a working representation of it. *Ta-da*: we 'see' a mucky blue bottle or a yellow, dishwasher-safe 8oz cup, and this is how we go about our lives from day to day, navigating our way in a real world through images produced by and held in our brain. And we speak more or less easily of this: we can quickly understand it is only a *representation* of the coffee cup with which the soft matter in our head is supplying us. But in that case, we can know nothing about the original cup that disturbed our sensory apparatus to begin with. We talk as if it were the real cup that started the process, triggering our brain to see or feel some subjective working version of itself, from one perspective at a time, as we move around it. But whatever truly exists in that 'real', noumenal world to create its recognizable ghost-image of a cup must by its very nature remain unperceived, unidentified. So it makes no sense for me to talk of what I see as a *representation* of a cup, as if it refers back to the original in the way that a drawing of a ball refers to a real ball, because I can't say *anything* about whatever started the process. Even to talk of it being 'an object' seems to be going round in circles. To presume the existence of a real cup kicking it all off is a complete leap of faith. The Phenomenological movement in philosophy insists that for that original 'thing' to be a cup, for it to exist in any meaningful way, it implies us, a perceiving subject.

The normal model of perception thus proposes a 'real' world and then strips it of any consequence. Literally, it is meaningless. The meaning of a thing comes from the relationship it has to us, which in turn is dependent upon our perceptions and memories, the way we use the objects in question, and the ever-changing context in which those objects appear. Meanwhile, that postulated, supposedly 'real' world that lies beyond all subjectivity is not so much real as an *abstraction*. We talk of cold scientific objectivity, forgetting that the scientific method relies on our senses (such as observation and intuition) to conduct its experiments and form its conclusions. Our sensory immersion in the world consistently muddies the supposed separation of perceiver and perceived.

Over time, the familiar model of our relationship to the 'real' world has settled alongside our vision of the self as a remote unit, housed inside a body (probably in the head), forever mysterious to others and permanently estranged from goings-on outside. Two thousand years ago, Plato founded Western thought with a vision that drove a wedge between Inside and Out. He flung Truth far beyond anything we could hope to touch with our bodily experience, out beyond the horizon, and into a hazy golden realm of immortal Ideals. Thus, in our lived experience we might meet the ordinary, flawed examples of such things as beauty or trees or rivers. But *out there* existed the true, capitalized form of perfect Beauty or Tree or River, in a place we could only reach through dry philosophical contemplation. In the search for wisdom, we were taught to leave our bodies and other solid things behind. And at the same time we were shifting away from an embodied, oral culture, in which stories were lived and animated, and circular Time orbited the seasons and cycles of life and death. To take its place came a new culture of writing, and stories were wrenched from mouths and bodies and landscapes. Thoughts and tales could now be considered in abstraction, separated from the spoken here and now. The past could be held and examined. The circle of Time was broken and stretched lengthways, forming linear history.

Many of our anguishes may well come from the feeling of isolation created by a divorce of self from its surroundings, and the way we perceive things as separate from us – separate from our identity, which recoils and retreats to protect itself. By contrast, to stand in wonder before the world is to close the gap and immerse ourselves afresh in it.

Verbing

How, then, to find Wonder, if the experience of immersion must ditch two thousand years of existential isolation? Our egos, neatly ordering the cleaning cupboards of our psyches and forever threatened by disarray, have daily bolstered this two-world view, because if we are fundamentally severed from any direct experience of the world, then the arm's-length things in it feel easier to name and reduce. Nouns – labelled things – are easy to possess, to call our own. Once we have arranged them, we can close the cupboard door and move on, unbothered by complexity.

We might try transforming the Big Nouns in life to something more embodied and active – in other words, verbs. Shaken up in this way, concepts burst into life, and wonder may find space to emerge. It is verbs that move and slide beneath our feet while our ego frantically tries to organize them into motionless configurations of nouns. Happiness, Success, Failure, Love – these cause us too much heartache by presenting themselves as static and objective. Let's see them as verbs, things we *do*. We are actively engaged in how happy we are; the labels of success and failure belie a shifting relationship to

191

events as they unfold and as we compare them to our expectations; meanwhile, love must be found and animated each day in a hundred minor gestures. Even a bottle of polish, it turns out, needs our present and active involvement to bring it to life and give it any meaning. How much more involvement and activity might we find by *verbing* some of these concepts?

As a case in point, take the Environment. There is a fine example of a big noun that, in its neat formulation and self-contained stasis, detaches us from what should be a ready source of wonder. Why are we so absurdly reluctant to take care of the ground, life and air that support and sustain us? There are many reasons, not helped by how we don't like to feel nagged, and the fact that the damage being done happens too slowly to engage us. But deep within me I feel somehow separate from the shrewish and troublesome Environment *thing*, which seems to lie somewhere out *there*, abstract and unrelated to the land and air in which I intimately move and breathe. For this reason, it is most often those people who have seen first hand the collapse of the colossal glaciers or observed the extinction of species – those who have lived it, actively – who are staggered at the half-heartedness of the rest of humanity's efforts to salvage what's left. And those of us who have swum alongside the glassy giants of the tropical seas can surely, ever since, only view the ocean as something alive, kinetic and truly deep. The call must be to re-embed ourselves in this abstract 'environment', to re-verb this *thing*, to get it, as it were, re-verberating, pulsing with life. Once Environment is alive and active, I naturally zoom in on the busy work of insects, on the silent processes of plants, the soil's silent toil. Conceptually re-charged, it is abundantly clear that I rely on every part of its vitality to sustain myself. I feel it bonded to my body through my actions; I sense it beating here in *this* ground which I touch, in *this* air that sticks to my skin and moves across my tongue and teeth as I breathe and speak.

We are normally unaware of the shifting, verbing nature of reality. We live oblivious to that mutually dependent relationship between our perceiving inner selves and the world 'out there' of slippery things which decline to have meaning the moment we turn our back. Consider how we submit to the rules of institutions and traditions, as if they have an independent authority beyond our own choice to sustain them through our behaviour. There is a self-forgetfulness that characterizes this normal mode – a cousin of our busyness and an enemy of wonder. To remember who we are in relation to the world and enrich our relationship with it, we need to be more happily *unsettled*. Cosiness and predictability must be shaken up, and nouns undone, through an effort to see people and things as vital and active.

Strangely, as with melancholy, this might make anxiety an unexpected friend. Or to be precise, a subtle form of anxiety, that type which is normally about nothing in particular. The German phenomenological philosopher Martin Heidegger distinguished it from mere fretting or fear, which tend to seize upon clear objects like dentists and clowns. Instead, let us recognize that mood which can settle at any time, alone or in company, and occasions an awareness of a certain meaninglessness, a contingency, a lack of firm basis to anything. If our daily experience of a rich and captivating world is generally cosy and familiar – *heimlich* – then this anxiety instigates the sense of the *unheimlich*, the uncanny, the unsettling. Comfort retreats and an unfamiliar aspect reveals itself; the world may even be disclosed as an absurd domain of trivial activity. It is a form of anxiety that is entirely appropriate, given the fact that we exist at all. When we lose our footing in certainty, we have been ushered beyond the familiar line-up of static nouns and embedded into the less familiar territory of *process*, of verbs.

Back to magic for a moment. Sometimes the plots of magic tricks happen in real life, without any theatrical framing, and evoke bewilderment rather than wonder, or sometimes fail to register at all. For example, I have many times searched frantically for a pen and then found it in front of me, sitting dumbly where I had looked but not seen. *Voilà*: a conjured appearance, formally identical to a magic trick, but without wonder. Or its reverse: I am sure I just placed the same pen down a few moments ago, but now it has gone, and I am searching in exasperation for a vanished item. Perhaps I shall find it has rolled away, silently and unseen, and come to an improbable rest behind the base of my desk lamp. Or maybe I never placed it down and I am misremembering. Again, these are all tools of the magician: obscuring, transporting, creating false memory. But I am not delighted by the results, only frustrated. The difference may lie in the fact that when a magician performs the same trick, I am forced to face a fact: that *something complex has been made to happen in the world to which I have not been privy*. If that is the difference that makes the difference, then perhaps it resonates because I must accept a slippery world outside, and one that can be manipulated by others who have their own aims and agency. The theatrical vanishing of a pen, if it is done well and triggers a kind of wonder, makes me, in my sudden smallness, apprehend the largeness of what is outside of myself, and therefore the motivations, the *otherness*, of others. The mere loss of my own pen does not hint at such riches, and my bewilderment will only point me towards frustration. But with a good magician in control, the world can shift from a place of closed and comfortable nouns, *things* that we watch carefully (pen, table, hand), to the openness of a verbing mystery (*What did he do? What has happened that I don't know?*).

Perhaps, then, there is a particular form of wonder in the apprehension of the agency of otherness. Such agency could easily spell threat rather than wonder, so, like Burke's Sublime, it demands distance. The theatrical parenthesis around a magician's performance lends us that remove, and we know that no one who possessed the ability to transgress the laws of thermodynamics would use the same to make a biro vanish.

Our ever-present inclination is to react against the strangeness of what is separate from us: in short, the very thing that makes that other thing 'other'. The potential for threat that lingers in the unknown has us shore up our conservative impulse, like those lefties in our experiment who entered a disgusting room and, for a short while, failed their liberal ideals.

And apprehension at what might lurk in a dark forest has us strike up a cosy fire in a clearing to sit around and tell ourselves stories. Snug, smug and mellow, we curl up, unchallenged and immobile in the stories we tell, each one reinforcing the last. But we could also try to acknowledge the dark fringes of the clearing, and otherness where we find it. We can do this by keeping the verb-mode in mind, and letting its strange open-endedness have a resting place in us. And when we pause to do so, we might rekindle wonder.

That cup again: I reach and touch it with my thumb and first two fingers, to check if my coffee is still warm. Disappointingly, as before in New York, it has cooled: I had forgotten it, a little lost in editing the last few pages. But with coffee cups already on my mind, I think: *I have no idea what one feels like.* Do you? Do you know what a cup feels like? I know very well what it feels like *in my finger* to touch one, yes: cool and smooth. But that is a quality somehow from and in my finger, not the cup. What the cup feels like, rather than what my finger feels like when touching a cup, I have no clue.

And so I consider my partner, and how amid a deluge of daily duties I rarely take delight in his otherness, his mystery. I know the range of ways he makes *me* feel, but how rarely I pursue a valuable project: to find out what it must be like to be him. Not to judge him, not to meet every difference with fear and disappointment, not to find my way back home to nouns. Instead, to stumble across wonder; in venturing out, in discovering how he experiences life. I could begin to delight at the foreignness of his answers, and at the mighty otherness of this person whom I might spend a lifetime getting to know.

THE HIDDEN CLEARING

Two days ago I stood before my basement toilet, staring blankly at the tatty collection of books lined up on shelves behind the high-cistern pipe. I had never considered them as any sort of collection before. They amounted to fifty or so volumes way too low-brow to keep in my main library, many of them gifts accrued over decades whose hand-written, festive dedications had spared them a trip to the Heart Foundation. They had grown into a subterranean stockpile of ersatz paperbacks, most of them falling under the publishers' classification of 'Humour', along with some slim stocking-filler hardbacks that dealt with kooky topics such as cocktail-making, stone-skimming and book lovers' walks around London.

It was my task to decide, finally, those I could throw out. I was to take them to our local branch of Mailboxes Etc, which boasted a happy table of DVDs and books to which customers could help themselves. We were about to move house, to get out of London, and it was time to tackle the toilet library. I leafed through a blue volume, Shaun Micallef's *Smithereens*, and read the sweet words penned by an Australian friend who had been keen for me to discover his native comic favourite. Next to it *Crap Taxidermy, The Meaning of Liff, Pets with Tourette's*. Keep all those. Rearranging a few, I realized I had unwittingly accrued the entire collection of Woody Allen's comic prose anthologies, in a now unhygienic set of first editions. Armando Iannucci's *Facts and Fancies* – keep those too. Robertson Davies's *The Papers of Samuel Marchbanks*, decades ago dropped into the loo whereafter the slimmish paperback had distended and dried into a crinkly, bloated mass that had swollen so far around itself that its own spine was barely visible. I'd kept that one because I liked how it had deformed, but now I must be brutal. I felt the sting of twenty-five years as I placed it on the discard pile: I had been gathering these books since my student years. There too were all the *A Bit of Fry and Laurie* scripts with the duo's faces fresh and taut on the cover, pages thoroughly thumbed and suffering from too many years in unpalatable air.

Something made me picture the new home to which we were moving: a country place with Tudor beams and low ceilings, which would take work to keep from looking chintzy. Then, as I considered these books – musical reviews by George Bernard Shaw, the *Viz Profanisaurus* – I imagined them on the shelves at that house. And *that's* what did it. Quite suddenly, as I stood there, facing my lavatory in a very familiar way, just three days before my fiftieth birthday, they *flipped*. Changed. And along with them, the whole world. There was a moment before it happened, when they still were that familiar collection of old volumes and memories, a homely backdrop of affectionately relegated relics. And then, in an instant, as I pictured them in the bathroom of their new home, a nausea descended. They became, horrifyingly, *an old man's collection of books*. And so I stood and stared.

The transformation of my university-era library of funnies into Grandad's weird old books destined for a skip only confirmed a suspicion that had been gnawing at me for a year or so. It was something I had already noticed in relation to my cardigans. I have always enjoyed an old-man woolly, but worn them with the whiff of trendy irony one would expect from any east London prick. I had started to don them at around the age of forty, by no means in the first bloom of my ruddy youth's springtide, but neither did it seem fair that I should topple incontinent into the grave because of a soft spot for front-fastening woolwear. But of late, unquestionably in the incontestable core of the nucleus of the epicentre of middle age, I have had to acknowledge that my muted cardigans are a grey area. *Vintage* no longer reads as a choice. It is many years since I stopped noticing I was generally the oldest person in any coffee-shop, and a handful since I started to question the authority of anyone in their twenties about anything. Most of my passing crushes now read as creepy. My brilliantly wry interjections in conversation now sound, I fear, like Dad-jokes. My partner recently admonished me for my Use of Humour with waiters, and as I silently despaired at my fate, my heart plunged beneath the neckline of my cashmere-blend shawl-collar button-up. (Being well known makes it very hard to judge your own quips: if there is one constant to the experience of fame it is that people laugh way more than they should at your jokes.) Something, I had been thinking of late, was happening, and the fright of the accumulated nineties book-spines carried the clear message that it had already occurred.

Midlife, and the spectre of mortality that it ushers in, creates a stubborn, bewildering form of friction for many. With that in mind, here follows a meandering through its mechanisms, to perhaps help us find some solace within it. It is a time when the soul yearns, but it's not always clear what is struggling to be articulated.

What has changed? In the first half of our lives, particularly young adulthood, our ego is in a sustained dialogue with, principally, the outside world. While I was collecting most of these books, I was, like many, forming my career, looking largely to external affirmation as my guide, and planting my sense of self somewhere *out there*, in the rocky, precarious ground of approval and status. At such an age, we find our environment offers a constant influx of endorsement and rejection, and a stream of clues as to how well we are faring in comparison to others. It is our task of sorts to make something of ourselves, find our place, our partner, and stake our claim. All of this relies on verification from the outside world, and thus we benefit from being well attuned to its communications. And of course this is still the case even if we self-consciously reject what we take to be the world's values: as I have said elsewhere, *fuck you* is too much about the *you*.

When we were infants, we had no choice but to internalize our parents' behaviours, along with the unconscious messages and implications that accompanied them. We had no choice but to interpret it all as unchallenged information about ourselves and the world. This is the misjudged sense of specialness from one too young to know any better. A related feeling usually continues in some form through childhood: we commonly aspire to have exciting jobs when we are grown up, or to be famous. Thus our immersion in a dialogue with the world is maintained, along with our concern for our place in it. And then, when we are old enough to break from our parents, we quickly seek parent substitutes: figures of authority and nurturing characters, more beacons from the world to guide our way. We soon learn to engage in a certain theatre of the self – a performance of sorts, a mode of meeting others and a way of presenting an increasingly honed character which we sometimes practise in private. Others do the same, and the play continues. The Instagram feed, that theatrical curation of triumph, is no more a sad sign of modern decline than is the proliferation of the selfie: as we flick through ten near-identical shots for that perfect one to post, we are merely continuing a lifelong predilection for calculated social staging. The modern, snooty distaste for selfies may be due to their laying bare the performative aspect of our own selves to which none of us likes to admit.

Keeping us engaged in this ongoing conversation with the world and the battles and prizes it proposes, young adulthood

brings a heroic mode to life. We have become the bold protag-
onists of our stories, forging what feels like our blazing path.
But our compass is less than reliable, and we turn out to be a
cluster of over-sensitivities. Thus we head off boldly a few
degrees off-target, and before long we are trudging through
brambles and thickets, far from any unimpeded path.

We're unaware our guidebook has been written by our parents and others who are clearly strangers to this particular
part of the forest. We overreact to the dangers we sense in the
woods, we change track when we should tenaciously continue
forward, we blindly forge ahead when we should have diverted
long ago. We bring to bear our hopeless over-generalizations
about the horrors that lurk around us. As best we can, we
stumble onwards, flag held high – or anxiously hidden.

Midlife tends to bring a natural end to this heroic quest.
Arriving at a clearing not shown on our map, we may note with
disappointment that we haven't travelled very far, and often
round in circles. We neglected to explore alternative paths, and
it may feel too late to embark on new adventures: we were only
allocated the one. If we found a companion along the way, they
no longer seem to be the person they once were. We are lost,
unsure why, and no one we meet seems able to help. As we step

into the clearing, our heroic role is relinquished, and we will be humbled.

But we will not be brought to our knees quietly. Our understanding of the world – the world upon whose terms we have formed our identity – is collapsing, so we may panic. We might try to destroy all we have and know. Or perhaps there is just a creeping sadness, and a vague sense of resentment towards our partners. Perhaps (ho ho) we have lost a parent, or at least have watched them grow enfeebled, and in facing their mortality have been brought up against our own. The ground around us is slipping. Those Big Nouns we took for granted – Security, Family, Relationship, Satisfaction – are losing their hard and clear edges. They are revealed to be active verbs, choices that we realize we play a major part in shaping and maintaining. No longer will they fall into place on their own. Some may face this uncertainty by developing a new mode of intolerance, in a last-ditch attempt to calcify moral attitudes which are under threat from inside and out. We may also become aware of a kind of drudgery, a disappointment regarding nothing in particular.

What has happened to us? Writing these words at fifty with a thoughtful approach to happiness, unrestrained by the usual demands of having a family, and with a varied job I have managed to push and pull into different areas I enjoy, I hoped I would be immune to the common languishing of middle age. I think I have so far managed to avoid much of its disquiet, but other aspects are unquestionably familiar. Sometimes it seems to be that very familiarity which is most disappointing. What a shame to find oneself susceptible to the normal hollows of life: breaking up, being lonely and sour, needing help. How disappointingly *ordinary*. How *vulnerable*.

A likely culprit: the optimism of youth may well have caught up with us. In our earlier, valorous life, our ambition is buttressed by the shimmering mirages of our goals and other phantoms. This necessitates a hopeful outlook: it is normal to imagine, as we move through young adulthood, *that our situation will be better a few years from now*. But during our forties we are likely to rein in that sanguine spirit. Gradually, we come to realize that we are simply where we are: that we have approached the castles in the air and most simply dissolved. Perhaps, if we're lucky, we are doing well in the eyes of the world or have ticked off some major goals we wanted to achieve. But even if this is the case, we may now struggle to find the pleasure in precisely those kinds of achievement. We know they are supposed to make us feel grateful and content, but they're not having the right effect. Whichever way it comes, the optimism that drove us forward has been gradually eroded by the crashing waves of reality.

Allied to this, we find another self-sabotaging aspect of ourselves, which gets us in the end. It relates to the way we view ourselves and gauge our success. When we think forward a few years and picture ourselves in a better position, we are making a comparison of our *present self* with our *future self,* and this provides us with our sense of purpose. But when those few years have passed, and if we now enjoy that improved standing, what do we do? Do we look back to our younger self and feel happy that we have moved forward? Very rarely. Instead we look around our peer group *now,* and compare ourselves with those *who are doing a little better than us.* And again we find ourselves lacking. This unhappy trick of our nature keeps the cycle of motivation going, and thus it may well serve an evolutionary purpose. But over time it will inspire us less and less. Sooner or later – and usually around those mid-forties – the optimistic mindset that served us is likely to strike us as futile.

We need answers to our bleak conundrum. They exist, and some are hidden in plain sight. How, then, might we tackle this period of transit in our lives, endure it as easily as possible, and emerge most happily?

Firstly, let us *be aware of its routine nature*: aware of it coming, aware of its presence, aware of the likelihood of malaise, of emptiness and struggle, in whatever overt or subterranean form they arrive. The cliché of a midlife 'crisis' is misleading, as it suggests a sudden, dramatic nosedive. It is rarely that, and has led some psychologists to call it out as a myth. But if we think of it instead as a kind of despondency that creeps upon us, then we can accept that it is *the normal human experience of midlife* (I hear even apes have been shown to suffer from it). Then, more or less comfortable that it is part of the normal progression of life, we can accept that despite appearances, we are at least neither mad nor bad for experiencing it. If you have everything of which you ever dreamt surrounding you and still you feel empty, or like running away, or find you resent those who love you the most, *you are normal.*

This is another case where the sting of personal tragedy can give way to a gentle, appropriate, outward-reaching melancholy. The real problem is that we are offered no guidance as to how to navigate through this time, rather than the cruelty of the time itself. We have likely emerged into a sense that many of our strategies are no longer rewarding, that we are not in charge in quite the way we would like, that something is slipping away. Frustration, blame and destruction will be normal responses if we are not offered solutions. What continues here is an offer of counsel for those of us emerging into the clearing. Or, a pre-emptive strike for those of you too young to believe that it awaits, but who will nonetheless require a fresh map on arrival.

So, having acknowledged its normality, here is a second thought. We may faintly sense that we have been deflected from our *true path*, because of the faulty nature of our naviga-tional tools and that relentless need to be planting our flag somewhere. It may feel like our principal social and profes-sional goals have been realized, but at the expense of our happiness, or of our 'authentic self', whatever that might be. So a question for this time is: if we hadn't internalized this or that misguided belief about ourselves, if we hadn't sought certain rewards or worked so hard to avoid unnecessary terrors, where might we have headed? What was the authentic path we never trod? *What are we supposed to be doing?*

Of course the question is a trick. It makes no sense to posit, let alone chase after, some alternative version of ourselves. We are only who we are because of the choices we made at each

step along the way. To even call them real *choices* may be a mis-
nomer: who can say why the winds have brought us here or
there, or what forces restricted our options and influenced our
decisions at each moment? But imagine that there was some
potential at the start, some nascent version of ourselves that
was gradually lost to those fatal, infantile over-generalizations
we formed in the face of the world. What might that young
person have become? Had we been immune to the manifold
sources of propaganda and misinformation that created the
over-sensitized and prickly version of ourselves we now are,
how might we have emerged? What would we be doing now?

We can never answer the question, but there is value in playing the game and looking for useful clues. Where might we find
them? In those activities that bring us, in midlife, the most joy.
Of course the interests we have are in truth inseparable from
the quirks and needs of the misaligned being we have grown
into. But they commonly speak of a more integrated version of
ourselves, and this might well be at odds with the demands and
expectations of grown-up life. Also, as we identify what brings
us delight, we can be less preoccupied – as many are in midlife –
with what our 'purpose' might be. In place of this common
concern, we can focus on simply developing our talent at

whatever excites us the most, be it painting or parenting. And we can pay particular attention to areas where our different passions converge; it is into those crossover places we might choose to pour most of our efforts. They will be peculiar to us, and especially worthy of our attention.

As we lean into what brings us joy rather than continuing to elevate recognition and status, so we can accept that midlife should involve a readiness to change, or at least develop, our direction. The notion of 'purpose' tends to be tethered to the world, and misses the point of a distinction which we can now start to consciously recognize. Our new task is to shift our pre-occupation from *how we fit in the world* to *how we fit with ourselves.*

We can start to pick apart the flawed intelligence which has caused our problems and sent us astray. What are the recurring problems in our lives that might point towards a common source, and where could their origin lie within ourselves? The parts of us we bury, remember, gain a certain energy and frequently re-emerge to cause damage. When they do, they tend to appear like *external* problems of the world, such as repeated difficulties in our relationships. (A clear example of this at work is the person who buries a strong homosexual urge, pursuing a straight marriage in order to present an 'accept-able' persona to themselves and others. What destruction awaits in that couple's world.)

By midlife, our strategies seem to have worn thin. Many, we see now, despite being hard to shed, are childish and outdated. What created them? What were we seeking? What approval? What protection? We have built a life around needs born from an understandable misunderstanding of the world. Now it is time to rotate the axis of that dialogue and form a new one with our inner lives, and the authentic self with which we have lost touch.

Here is the strange fact: we may live through an entire life without ever appearing as ourselves. Until now we have led an existence shaped by a conglomeration of wishes: our own, those of our parents, those of the many forces which have pressed upon us. We have hung on to our childish attitudes and avoided so many opportunities for growth. The grand oppor-tunity of midlife, and of the wide space offered by that clearing, starts with finding what we actually want for ourselves.

As it is, this might sound like an encouragement to end a marriage, have the affair, destroy the present to reclaim the past. What is adultery at this point other than an attempt to recover what has been lost? Our partners, after all, seem to have changed. When we met, in the earlier flush of young adulthood, we were still projecting upon them our needs, forming them in our image. As we both grew, our diverging demands created tensions and resentment. If one partner forfeited their career, concentrating instead on raising the family, they may now feel underdeveloped, under-confident in the marketplace to which they may now wish to return, unsure of what they can offer but eager for change. Stable relationships, in which partners can stand guard over the solitude of the other and accommodate these rumblings with ease, are not common. So should we strike a death blow to the relationship to recover what we feel is an authentic self?

Well, no; I am not championing destruction. Identifying what we want is only part of the answer. When we know what is being articulated by the supposed midlife crisis, there is no need to throw spouse and babies out with the domestic bathwater. To begin with, we should allow changes to happen incrementally, without sudden disruption. Moreover, when we find out what we need, we can aim to bring that better self back to those we love. This process, called 'individuation' by C. G. Jung, is never a summons to destructive narcissism. Our principal question is

changing from *Where am I in the world?* to *Where am I in myself?* –
but *this is a self that is rooted in social connections.* So we can
orientate that developing self outwards, to serve a social purpose. We are not going to grow by fetishizing self-regard and
destroying whatever challenges it. Instead we can catch ourselves in the mirror, by seeing what brings our best self out into
the light.

This brings us to the third question we can ask: *To what now
can I be of service?*

It is important, if we wish to avoid the horrors of a dis-
orientated middling chapter of life, to start to think beyond
ourselves. *What is larger than me, in which I can lose myself?*
That is, after all, how we find meaning. Finding value in our
own heroic struggle has run its course. Now, with the fine
symmetry of paradox, our new conversation with our selves is
likely to be most enriched by looking beyond ourselves for
significance. In Jung's words (and he seems to have been the
first psychologist to recognize the importance of the midlife
passage), 'The first half of life is devoted to forming a healthy
ego, the second half is going inward and letting go of it.'

It might help to imagine that vertical line, which we have
been climbing for so long – a career ladder, or a striving

towards a goal. During this time, our loved ones may have found themselves on the sidelines. Sometimes they have felt like – to us and/or to themselves – a drudge, an inconvenience, a weight attached to us as we tried to climb. Now we can find the present point on that line – where we are now – and spread it out, horizontally. We might imagine that our experience of the world, rather than pushing singly up and forward, reaches instead sideways to include more fully those things that are already with us, such as our relationships, our children, the ways in which we are of use to others. It is helpful to pay more attention to those activities which do not serve us in the future. They have no *telos*, no objective other than the pleasure and richness of experience they offer in and of themselves. It is these activities which we might choose to seek out and prioritize, day by day. We can broaden our interests to include *this present*, and those who already share it with us.

How little we understood, as we surged forward in the first half of life, that it was usually the engagement of the journey that offered all the rewards, and rarely the enjoyment or emptiness of arrival (especially if the destination kept shifting further into the future), let alone the generic trappings of success. The rewards of goal-achievement may have been no more profound than taking a rest after an enjoyable period of travel. If that is true, then we spend much of our lives trying to bring to completion the very activities which bring us most pleasure. Midlife offers us a new agenda: instead of an increasingly panicked race against mortality to improve upon our achievements, we can allow more space for the richer rewards of the here and now.

It is within this context that we can seek out our passions, and listen to the cries of our forgotten, lost selves. We might pay attention to times of easy delight – of flow and spark and excitement – as pointers towards what is yearning to be reclaimed by our adult selves. But we can also understand: our self is not a selfish thing, it thrives in a network with others. So we can discover these reclaimed aspects of ourselves *within the context of our relationships*.

After having fought our valiant battles of the self, we might now look back and feel that in our youth we were oddly dislodged from life and who we were. Too busy working, too busy comparing ourselves to others, too busy chasing things which now feel less important than they did. Our goal now might be to make sure we are fully present in the world, that we have our eyes open and are engaged with the stuff of living our life. As we pay attention to what truly animates us, and as we reach out to find more meaning in what is larger than us, then opportunities for engagement with others will present themselves more readily.

The alternatives? Some destroy the lives of those around them, while many more never truly claim the one they have.

So far, then, we can gently:

- accept the normal pattern of our situation (and not make things worse by thinking ourselves bad);
- pay attention to what activities, in and of themselves, bring the richest rewards to our soul (and pay less attention to the shrill voices of ambition and status);
- let our sense of who we are lean more generously into our relationships, and look to serve what is greater than us (because our time for ego-serving has run its course).

Perhaps above all we lack a rite of passage, or at least a sympathetic social narrative. Consider, by means of contrast, adolescence. It only appeared as a social category at the start of the twentieth century; the early half of the nineteenth saw no accepted period of adjustment for young people between education and work. Today, we understand, with varying degrees of sympathy, that teenagers are in a sort of holding pattern between one stage of life and another, that the way through may be bewildering and challenging for them. Some will have an easier time than others, but it is a pardonable time of attunement and we rarely seek recourse to mockery as we do when we snicker at the impedimenta of the Middle-Aged Man.

We think more charitably about adolescence because most of us are on the other side of it, thinking back across our own experiences, happy to forgive our former selves any trespasses. When we worry about middle age, however, we are *anticipating* it, and have not been vouchsafed such generous hindsight. It is as if we were to embark upon adolescence now, with the self-knowledge and open eyes of adults; with the queasy sense of everything we have constructed until this point being called into question; with the horizon of our mortality present and visible; and embedded in a culture that provided us with merciless caricatures of what this coming period would look and feel like. And when we tried to look beyond the upcoming passage, instead of seeing a world of functioning adults we could perceive only a shapeless, grey winding-down of life. We lack the benefit of perspective from which the languors of midlife might be upheld as the forgivable symptoms of a temporary period of transit. As with adolescence, that perspective – or wisdom – must come from those who have travelled through.

Finally, then, the narrative we most need may be provided for us by Jonathan Rauch's 2018 book *The Happiness Curve*. Surprisingly, the game-changing insight has been gleaned not from the close-up work of psychologists but from the arm's-length stance of economists picking through the big data of nationwide and global statistics on happiness. Jonathan describes a strikingly reliable pattern unearthed by these surveys as well as from the several hundred interviews he carried out himself. There is an 'undertow' of difficulty that we are very likely to face in our forties, though how it manifests will of course vary greatly from person to person (like adolescence). Our optimism all but runs out and worldly success may beget only a baffled shame at our own incapacity to experience gratitude. But – and here is the revelation we need – *we get happier once we're through it.* There is a U-shaped curve to our happiness that declines towards midlife and soars again thereafter.

This upswing is supported by the very fact that our expectations have stalled in midlife. The unrealistic optimism of youth has carried us forward; disappointing setbacks in our twenties felt inconsequential, as so much time stretched before us. After a while we probably started to recognize them as part of the structure of life, and became aware of an increasing undercurrent against which we had to push. Around our forties and into our fifties, we may feel run aground. But *after* that period, 'For a good twenty years, every year brings, not another dose of regret and disappointment, but another pleasant surprise. So there is the undertow, and its reversal. The forecasting errors that bring so much grief in the earlier part of life switch sign in the latter portion. The current shifts.'

Much of Rauch's book is devoted to showing how reliable this curve is, across nations and cultures, reflected among his interviewees and even those apes. Even when other possible contributing factors to well-being are taken into account, the pattern of time and ageing holds. As our outlook and values change, life gets worse before getting better.

Rauch's most unusual piece of advice, then, which I add here to my own, is to *wait*. We are undergoing 'a slow-motion reboot of our emotional software to repurpose us for a different role in society'. The clearing I have described provides us with the opportunity for something like Jung's individuation (a move towards a fuller self) that points us, in more integrated form, outwards into our relationships. This is tantamount to wisdom, which emerges as the project of later life. Rauch suggests there may be an evolutionary resonance to this turn of events: more or less past child-bearing age, our role is now shifting towards what serves our tribe.

Be that as it may, the recommendation of patience seems like excellent advice, although he only offers it as part of the programme. Seeing our place in a human happiness-curve, unearthed by data impossible to identify in the close-up stories of varying individual lives, might provide us with a perspective as helpful as our hindsight regarding adolescence. Of course, difficulties to come will always loom larger than those in our past. Such are the different weights of past and future. Our non-existence before we were born does not feel as worrying as the one that awaits us after we die, even though it amounts to the same thing. But to know that just as we suffer now during this 'reboot' we will find surprise and greater happiness when we emerge – this might be the lifeline we need. With its beginning, middle and end, the course of that U-shape gives us what we require when we are lost: a good story in which to find ourselves; the resonance of myth rediscovered.

PRIVATE VISIONS:
ALONE AND TOGETHER

A few years ago, in defiance of my partner's urgent petitions, I found myself resistant to buying a second dog. Unlike my hesitation the first time around, this was not about the ethics of purchasing a pooch. My pause came from somewhere deeper, and surprised me with its quiver of existential alarm.

Our pre-existing dog was Doodle, with whom you are already acquainted. A country cross-breed, she is wilful, indifferent to affection, and happiest when carrying out the vital work of snoring or vomiting. Her chief tool is her tracker's nose – we call it her 'instrument', as in *she's got fox shit up her instrument again.* This organ has revealed to me a world of urban street food I had no idea existed. She has led me for half a mile in pursuit of a jettisoned tampon, and once smoothly ducked behind a Hackney bus stop to eat a human turd without breaking stride. With the deep-chested and persistent bellow of a brave protector we have been defended from attacks by recycling collectors, squirrels, bicycles, children with hats, children without hats, people with bad posture, beetles, fallen leaves animated by isolated eddies of wind, and, awkwardly, our neighbour with the Afro.

Serpent-breathed and racist as she may be, this tracking hound is thankfully neither soppy nor trendy, unlike many of the cockapoos and Frenchies which lollop and snort at the heels of east London coffee-grabbing hipsters. I enjoyed being *seen* with her: there is to me something appealing in the solitary no-nonsense aura of a hound which cannot be found in that of a terrier or lapdog, and I suppose I was happily signalling a vision of myself I liked. It was as if we were a *unit*.

This thought was barely conscious, but rumbled deep as I whined to my partner: 'But I like just having Doodle. I like that it's sort of me and my dog.'

'But it's not you and your dog,' he protested. 'It's *us* and *our* dogs!'

There I was, three years into a relationship, and my self-image, caught in the mirror like this, was still of a single man. A moment's further consideration clarified the laughably inappropriate vision I had established of myself: an artist in his studio, dog asleep by his side while he paints. One who (I recalled Leonard Cohen) *travels light*, a *one-man guy* (Loudon Wainwright III) unencumbered by dependants who occasionally leaves his studio to read something dense and obscure in a café, chuffing at a Gauloise and accompanied by his devoted familiar (who snacks under the table on her separate order).

In the wallet which accompanies me when I travel abroad, I carry a favourite photograph: a small shot of me walking Doodle near my house. She's still a pup, and I'm trim enough and wearing a jacket I like; it's just the two of us. I had kept this like a talisman, evidence of a magical reality that has never existed in which I am untethered from all responsibility save My Dog (and My Art). It's a fantasy, made evident by the fact I asked my partner to take the photo when we were out together. But this chimera still resonates for me. In recent years I have made a good friend in the portrait artist Jamie Coreth, who seems to live precisely the enviable life I describe. He rents studios which seem to me exquisite, lives and paints in them, sleeps on the little mezzanines those places offer, and walks his excellent dog Turtle. When I first visited Jamie in his Victorian studio, which had been based on the footprint of John Singer Sargent's own atelier, I felt that aspect of myself yearning to be realized. Our friendship has progressed largely on that basis.

Two dogs, though, in all of this, represented something else entirely. No reclusive but fascinating artist would own two dogs. There is no sense of a *unit*, no untouchable self-containment on display, when a strolling man has more than one dog (or has a single but stupid dog, like a chihuahua in a coat). *Two* dogs means a *family*. Walking two dogs means *it's my turn to walk them – there is someone else in my life to whom I am tethered.* Something in me recognized this and, shamefully, I reacted against it.

I *have* lived the solitary life, albeit with a parrot rather than a dog. My twenties were shaped by singleness, painting and the strangeness of personality that comes from rarely needing to make compromises. That decade's mood was a product of several forces, including those of an unusual job, and a history of having played alone as an only child until the age of nine (and largely alone thereafter as a substantially older brother). When we have long diverted ourselves in isolation, we carry such self-sustenance into adulthood. And if for whatever reason we were made to feel like outsiders as children, how fiercely we defend that identity as grown-ups. Thus Lego and drawing have given way to the stabilizing but unsociable pleasures of reading, writing, painting and photography, however much I enjoy the cosy stuff of coupledom.

This exchange about a second dog stayed with me, as it highlighted a tension of which I had not been consciously aware. It is a battle evident in the psyche of many partnered people, and especially so in midlife. It shows itself, even within a happy long-term relationship, in the crystal-clear desire *to be left alone.* To be allowed to work undisturbed, to perhaps write or paint or just sit at the computer, to think or nap or to choose to spend a day as one requires. To let things live where one has left them; to visit friends alone without guilt; to be who one is, without that being a daily source of irritation to someone else. The desire to be left alone can arise as a still small voice or a bothersome, bass, background beat, or quite suddenly as a scream of horror. But who can deny its presence?

I am blessed with a partner who is creative, generous and understanding. Yet how ugly is my almost persistent silent wish for more space to think and do. As much as I love him, I still experience a visceral thrill when I awake remembering that he has gone away for the weekend to leave me to my desk and studio.

I have, since my twenties, identified this solitary urge with the Nietzschean edict, borrowed in turn from the Greek poet Pindar, to 'Become who you are'. I used to read Nietzsche in a cave near my home in Bristol, caped and inexcusable, and phrases such as this would fill me with foolish young fire. But I still feel its urgency: to honour some authenticity within, to seek it above all else, and to find the dedication and space such a calling demands. It is a demand to spurn all compromise in matters of the soul. It is, in my case at least, grandiose and embarrassing to describe. And it is a vertical, forward-lurching urge, pulling those of us who feel it towards some irresistible but obscure horizon.

As that thought rises to consciousness, others follow. Firstly, the faint memory of when I was last single. Some delightful, sometimes rude, times; but also those unbecoming claws through Tinder, long vacant evening sadnesses on the couch, the empty, jeering fridge. Little memory of either painting or writing. The worry that with no one to love, one's soul might wilt.

And then there are those moments when the beam of my spotlight crosses and completely aligns with his, illuminating our shared space as the rest of the world melts into darkness. Such as today, when he took a nasal trimmer to my ears because he saw old-man hairs and didn't want me going out like that. When we're shopping and he nudges me to get something nice for my mum. When he organized not one but two surprise parties for my birthday. The knowledge that we are both (much of the time) happy to risk spending much of our lives with each other. The unlikely fact that each of us might be enough to make the other feel he has sufficient space in this world to flourish. Surely there, in that connection, despite the protestations of my younger self, is a better place to be found. Leaning into the in-between.

This is the horizontal urge that seeks to placate the Nietzschean vertical. Find who you are in your current relationships and compromises. Be completed by partnership and family. Take your eyes off the horizon: the better version of yourself will be found here already, tempered and shaped by the requirements of responsibility and sharing. How might this sit comfortably with the yearning to realize some unadulterated vision of my identity?

Well, firstly I think I misunderstood my Nietzschean ideal. He was not advising that we define a specific, authentic self, positioned out on the horizon, and then claw our way forward to claim it. Which is good to know, as such an idea falls prey to the same problems we find with much goal-setting and deferred, contingent notions of happiness. My weird urge to, say, be an artist and live alone (with a dog) quickly reveals a set of attendant problems. Principally, I am taking a single aspect of myself that I happen to like now and expanding it like foam to fill the entire space of a life and across all time, when I am better advised to keep my life fluid, in flux. It appeals now because it became something I took for granted in my twenties, and part of me misses the freedom of movement I had then. It's just a feeling that's still sticking around. My friend Jamie, too, is in his early thirties. But when I project that lifestyle forward to my sixty- or seventy-year-old self, alone and painting, it is not a happy picture. In the image I form, if I am honest, I am insufferable and no one really wants me over for Christmas. I have aches and pains from time spent at the easel (I already exercise to avoid back twinges exacerbated by standing waggling one arm all day) and no beloved encourages me to take care of myself. I am unable to sustain a romantic relationship because I am already wedded to an image of myself as a creative genius that leaves no room for others. I am a ghost . . . and this is what I would wish to become? Moreover, to live out such an aesthetic delineation of a life could fall prey to what that giant of existential philosophy Jean-Paul Sartre called 'bad faith': an insincere existence in which one plays out a part in the same way a waiter inhabits his role. It could be fundamentally inauthentic, not what anyone would wish to become.

Instead, Nietzsche was pushing for something closer to the Jungian notion of individuation. He was encouraging us to engage consciously with our development, to value the totality of ourselves and of our world. We should, he would advise us, question everything, live dangerously, and above all find meaning in self-knowledge. Mostly we just 'run through life as if [we] were drunk and once in a while fall down a staircase'. By becoming more conscious of ourselves, we apply our *will*: we create value and fashion our futures. This deliberate engagement with a fuller self is similar to the path that Jung envisioned for what he called 'the second half of life'. The process is the key, not the destination.

Earlier in this book I wrote about honouring ambiguity by synthesizing conflict. Here, then, we find such an opportunity to fuse the understandable desire for solitariness and 'becoming' with an opposing value – that of pre-existing relationships. The need to be left alone to live out a vision for ourselves can be of enormous merit. It might represent a demarcation of the soul, a way of reclaiming ourselves when we feel overwhelmed. But such needs are often born of panic: they tend to be triggered by fear in the face of deluge rather than the open-heartedness and tolerance of ambiguity that accompany us on the path to a fuller self. Not coincidentally, we are on similar ground to that of recent chapters on middle age and the tension of inner and outer.

John Kaag writes about precisely this friction in his beautiful book *Hiking With Nietzsche*:

> I remember too vividly an argument with my ex-wife that terminated with three words that I screamed before slamming our front door: 'Let. Me. Be!' I now know what I actually meant: 'Get out of my way.' Let me find my immutable essence. Unfortunately, there is no such thing as an immutable essence, at least not in my world. And so I left, but I never found what I was looking for.

John's memoir-cum-philosophical-expedition is a deep dive into the apparent antagonism between self-becoming and the surrender of self into family. His book helped me find language for the friction I was feeling but had been unable adequately to articulate.

He and I met for supper, and we enjoyed a spirit of commiseration. How does he surmise this business of becoming who you are? He introduces the important point of synthesis. Firstly, he says, the *Who* is not something you find out there, in Nietzsche's Alps where he travelled twice to locate it, or off in the future. It is found *here* in everyday, mundane acts of becoming. Neither is there an enduring *You*: you are something that changes, and you arise in the business of change. He concludes a TedX talk to the applause of a middle-aged crowd with this: 'Maybe becoming who you are involves getting over who you think you should be.'

John encourages us in midlife to prepare to lose and find ourselves again: 'The enduring nature of being human is to turn into something else.' Again, this resonates with Jung: it is the mode, task and opportunity of individuation. And the pleasure of exchanging sympathies over a table in Manhattan pointed to another truth: we can synthesize much of the conflict, but we should be prepared to live with the residual tension. The two urges will never sit quite comfortably: the growth we are to seek will only happen through bruising. We always have to let go of what feels secure – our familiar, childish ways – to fully face the world as ourselves. I cannot and should not, often as I want to, continue to live out my twenties.

The process of growth is not only helped by the demands of romantic relationships but, I suspect, is a principal reason for their existence. Our partnerships are there to show us how to grow. This is why we shouldn't end them when our annoyance is born from the general problems of *being in one*. As I have said, the irritations and difficulties we experience are often clues to what parts of us need attention. Our reluctance to fol-low those clues may derive from a refusal to get over a precious and too-tightly-held vision of who we think we should be.

Letting go of our childish sense of self and truly integrating the presence of another leads us into a more fitting relation-ship with the world. The world in which we must live is 'where things have place, part and counterpart, I and the one different from me', offered Rainer Maria Rilke, the Bohemian-Austrian poet, a century ago. Through allowing this other person an authentic place in our life we are acknowledging that a reality exists outside of our story – that life is in truth ambiguous, multi-perspectival, and awash with contradictions. And these inconsistencies are vital to even the most loving union: note how we tend to construct our love for our partners best when they are absent; how finding them again comes often not through intimacy but through distance; and how we derive a peculiarly personal experience when we see them through the eyes of strangers. Letting go a little helps us desire.

Only by acknowledging the contradictoriness as the true nature of the world can we then recognize the same truth within ourselves, and arrange, with Rilke, 'our own interiority with its internal contrasts and contradictions generously, spaciously, and with sufficient air to breathe'. This is the heart of growing up: to grant contradictions sufficient airspace. And likewise in the second half of life: to honour our own inconsistencies. For all its domestic disappointments, and despite our precious sulking and protestations, a sustained relationship provides us with the means of maturation, through the reluctant, mandatory acknowledgement of another person's world. No surprise that partners can be a nightmare.

I note that there are periods when I am immersed in the 'togetherness' and feel none of this alone/together tension, and other times when I struggle and cannot recall the easy equilibrium. Neither side of the line permits access to the other. When I am in a stretch of wanting solitude, I am irritable and I quietly blame my partner for what feel like eternal incompatibilities. But observing that to and fro, I have learned that what has typically carried me across to the wintry side has been precisely my immersion in a project such as painting. What appeared to be *I sometimes find my relationship difficult because I often want to lose myself in solitary projects* revealed its more accurate nature: *my tendency to detach and immerse myself in solitary projects puts an understandable strain on my relationship.*

If a painting is progressing well, then my mood is good, but I would rather be left alone to continue. On the other hand, if the piece is not going well, I am miserable. But through some extraordinary lack of self-awareness it is hard to identify the painting difficulties as the source of my despondency. Instead, I mope around, and then quietly blame my partner for my misgivings when he complains. It seems that to solve the grudge of wanting to be alone, I need to lean into the relationship, not away from it.

Such tensions are forever with us, and only exacerbated by other factors that may be in the air (at the time of writing, the cloying pressures of a second lockdown). Answers may only come through a series of pragmatic minor measures that sometimes add up to make a whole. I now don't paint for hours without checking in or coming down from my attic studio to make tea and chat for a bit. Such measures amount to a perfectly reasonable compromise that in turn has created a much happier painting life.

On that note, and while I am not sparing you my blushes, you may be interested to learn of a few methods we use to address a myriad of domestic tensions. In our case, one of us quite enjoys an argument, and the other (me) hates them, so it is natural that we have found a compromise in some strikingly passive-aggressive solutions.

Such as: the use of song. We have a few household ballads, the sound of which, if you were to traverse our moat and press your ear to our single boarded window, might surprise you in its delicacy above the cacophony of approaching attack dogs. Performed in a striking falsetto by your steadfast author and the man post-mortem tabloid articles will refer to in time as my 'gay lover', I offer two of our favourite pieces here. To appreciate a measure of their poignancy, you will have to conjure for yourselves an image of the highly sexualized choreography that accompanies them, as they are belted out *full voice* to an original melody:

SOMEBODY DIFFERENT

I wish you were

Somebody different,

I wish you'd become

Somebody else.

I'd love your personality

To change in its entirety.

I wish you were, I wish you were

Somebody else.

And the punchy

MUST YOU BE LIKE THAT?

Must you be like that?

Must you be like that?

When the magic of melody does not cast her spell, we have discovered another means by which to announce our cavils and carps: the Sarcastic Apology. This works well for occasions when one feels under-appreciated.

Him [hanging head in shame]: I feel like such an idiot.

Me: Why? What happened?

Him: Don't be angry, it's just – I'm really sorry – it's just that I did all the washing up and then I didn't think and did all the drying up as well. I'm so sorry, don't be annoyed. I know you saw me bring all the laundry down this morning and I don't want you angry that it was too much for me to do all on my own.

I'm certain you'll sense its effectiveness. If not, you may wish to try this alternative, Prayer Time:

Me: Are you using the study later on?

Him: Um, not really – when?

Me: Just before bed? Could I have it to myself for five minutes or so?

Him: Yes of course, I'm not using it. [Long pause during which I remain silent, until he has to ask:] Why? What do you need it for?

Me: Oh I just wanted some private space for a bit. I wanted to pray up there – just to pray that you'll be less of a narcissistic pig. So I was just wondering . . .

Making someone laugh may be the most effective way to simultaneously air a grievance while (generally) avoiding an escalation into argument or exhausting gravitas.

Humbug, our second dog, now licks my face each morning
with breath that reeks of metal fish. On occasions when she's
uncommonly excited she tilts back her head and howls at such
a frequency that she shifts into a sustained operatic vibrato
which makes us weep with laughter. She has not, it turns out,
affected my ability to paint. Instead, she has added a measure
of joy to the lives of Doodle and my partner – and, I remind
myself, mine too.

FINDING A WAY

The move to the country brought with it a series of minor dramas which may never have been shared by those of you with a breezier taste in decor. During the process of unpacking, two small glass tanks containing a nineteenth-century pickled kitten and a similarly preserved octopus were placed upon an unsecured shelf. A moment later they flung themselves six feet and deconstructed violently upon an ancient floor tiled in the encaustic manner. The simultaneous smashes were quickly supplanted by twin waves of disgust. Firstly, the visuals: the small cat, once hovering dreamily in its greenish preserving fluid, now lay gross and exposed next to its bulbous, rubbery confrère. For an instant, I half expected them to move; freed from a century and a half of preservation, it seemed natural that the ghastly invertebrate would now roll blind and bloated towards the shelter of the sofa. But neither stirred: shorn of the strange beauty of their enclosure, they lay still on the glazed terracotta, the deadest things I'd seen.

The second, more powerful repulsion was triggered by the smell. The fourteenth-century hallway, which once accommodated great banquets and (the estate agent had implied with a hushed tone of confidentiality) *passing royalty*, now stank of formaldehyde. The effect of the vinegary embalming fluid is powerful – 'like someone is forcing a large piece of concrete down your throat,' observed one survivor on Quora. We held our breaths as we hoovered up the glass and mopped up what we could of the death on the floor. I banished the horror of their slumped, lumpy articulation by picking up the creatures and immuring them in a medium ziplock bag from Waitrose; contained thus, they were placed in what was deemed in the moment to be a working chest freezer but has since turned out to be a sort of prop freezer with an orange light. A month later, due to the difficulty of disposing of white goods, they are still there. Perhaps they have now succumbed to the natural process of decomposition, slowly inflating their bag like a foul balloon in a silver-lined coffin. I cannot open the freezer to check their condition after the stink that issued last time I tried. The stench from the clay floor has now subsided, but our

Dyson, despite its peppy promises about cleaning up after pets, still whirrs malodorous poison into heart and lungs every time we switch it on.

Doodle (while on the subject of pets) has quickly adjusted to country life. She has transformed from resentful urban pup into a strong countrywoman, finely attuned to the scent-trails of the wily fox and helping herself to badger-shit as if it were popcorn. Humbug, the idiot sister, dotes upon the older dog and looks to her to learn rural ways, in between barking at pine cones and wandering aimlessly into roads. And the sleepless strain of relocating our vast collection of furniture, books and objects into a strange new house after a year of lockdown brought many cold-blooded evenings and exhausted, needless arguments.

It is a huge and desolate effort to move house, and as many people have been fond of pointing out to me, it comes right after divorce in the list of The Most Stressful Things in Life. But somewhere aside from the misery of impatience and dissension there is another force which moves quietly and painlessly to the same end of securing a home. I felt it early on as I put a pot of pens on my desk in my new study (I am quite tickled to have a study) and thought *this is where my pens go: my home has a study where I will finish writing that book and it has pens and they go here.* Looking out of the window over said desk, I now see a rose garden where in London I saw a fat cat in a flat window, and though I remember standing in front of my toilet bookshelves, my heart sinking at the thought of turning into an old man, I also think *this is my garden and it has roses and I'll sit out there and that will become normal.* I have noticed a quiet stream of these gentle moments, which patiently carry uncertainty and disorder towards security and comfort: the effortless creation of one's place.

They exist in stark contrast to the wild bursts of energy spent in pursuit of the same objective: the unpacking and arrangement of fittings and paraphernalia to make this place home. Pain and anger, exhaustion and frustration are the commonplace results of this desire to create a relaxing space. First those boxes – the boxes that fill your house and the boxes that fill your dreams, the paper to pull out, the lost items to be found. After the comfort of setting out a bunch of your things and making the place feel like a half-home, there may be building work to be done, electrics to be rewired (or, in the case of this old house, all but *introduced,* like Nana to her first cortado). Then perhaps the decorating, the snagging, the nagging of builders and contractors to show up or at least communicate something of their opaque plans and figures. This is for ever until it feels like home. Yet as this process is endured, at the expense of sleep and domestic civility, it all seems to exist for a strange aspect of home-building: the impressing of others. If it were not for anticipated guests, who know you too well or too little to care how you arrange your belongings, there would be none of this fuss. It takes starting again in this way to realize, with a tang of shame, how much effort is spent signalling one's self-image to the world. If we knew for sure that guests would never come, and we would never be judged, how little we would settle for – a practical, comfortable space. Even here in the privacy of our supposed *sanctum sanctorum* persists the quiet mumble of dialogue with the other, and the desire for the to-and-fro game of connection.

So on the one hand, all this effort is spent in a deliberate, conscious pursuit of finding a home. And on the other, there is something gentle and tenacious, through which a true sense of home slowly forms of its own accord. The latter takes no effort, requires no one to impress. Instead, it simply finds home piece by piece in the happenstance of a pen-pot or the view of the garden. It demands neither the neurotic assembling of doodahs nor any concern as to what chalky hue others may have chosen to coat their kitchen cabinets. Instead it is as if a part of us that yearns to find a place to call ours extends with a sigh into this or that corner, anticipating a familiarity that is yet to come. It speaks to me of a resolute, unconscious *will*, which persists with a tireless singularity of vision that has no recourse to the busy, fevered fuss of our calculating and deliberate functions.

Schopenhauer as decorator. He wrote of a deep Will that forms the undercurrent of all things. A relentless, unwavering pursuit of goals that may have nothing to do with our conscious plans, and which lends us direction at every moment. And the Will we sense within ourselves carries with it the unique quality of being the only thing in the world we can truly experience directly. In contrast to those coffee cups that we can only observe, we are *inside* our will, and if we silence all else, we feel it pulling us forward.

Thus, on my kitchen window-sill sits a pot of basil which has taken well to her east-facing spot and flourished impressively. She reaches towards the sun and pulls energy into herself through the wide leaves she has grown for that purpose. Were someone to rotate her, she would imperceptibly, calmly, set about correcting herself and turn again. In this dogged, blind appetite there is an elementary echo of the Will we identify in our intentional human conduct. 'The great difference between the two', wrote Schopenhauer, 'concerns only the degree of the manifestation, not the inner nature of what is manifested.' The will-to-make-a-home is at work in the back-breaking ordeal of unpacking boxes. It is there in our labour. But it is also present in this impulse that arrives without deliberation. It persists through both, but in the silence of the last in particular we sense its quiet tenacity.

When I think of Will appearing through toil and also quietly and without fuss, I think of Rievaulx. If you pick your way through the ruins of that abbey, which ascends in a remote valley of the North York Moors, and if you choose a day that has brought few tourists to the spot, you might encounter the home-making Will in both its forms. The Cistercians who founded the abbey provided us with some of the most beautiful architecture we can find in this country. They contributed to the blossoming of the Gothic architectural era, fusing the density of the Norman style with the pointed arches and weightless rib vaults of Burgundy, where their order was founded. Thus unlike the flamboyances into which the Gothic style eventually over-ripened, Cistercians remained rooted in austerity, interested particularly in light rather than ornamentation. The soaring, pointing skeleton that forms the heart of Rievaulx – the abbey church itself – has in its prodigious frame an airiness (and air is now in particular abundance) and an upwards pull which betray the spiritual aim of the thirteenth-century building project: to lift us, as we step inside the nave, from worldly concerns to the incorporeal.

If you wish, and for no charge, you can enjoy an audio tour of Rievaulx and discover, courtesy of English Heritage, '900 years of fascinating history'. These types of narration, often under-girded by sound effects and stock music, aim to stir those who may, in silent dialogue with the past, remain otherwise unstirred. At Rievaulx, we are provided with a sympathetic stream of facts concerning how the monks lived and maintained this vast centre of learning, prayer and, surprisingly, ironmongery. We are brought into a state of active imagination, artificially enlivened with busyness and human interest and animation. Likewise at the top of the Empire State Building in New York, the articulations of 'Tony', a voice-artist's interpretation of a brash but unthreatening cab driver, kept me very much informed *and* entertained. But don those headphones and you will be denied the experience of truly being present atop what was once the second highest building in Manhattan, of allowing the elevated view of that delirious island to find its way into your private sphere, and above all the experience of perspective and peace in a galvanized metropolis formed of scaffolding and sound. The benefit of passive receptiveness and of allowing ourselves to be *worked upon*, which is the finest gift of Rievaulx and all great architecture, is lost in our neurotic obsession with interactivity.

Built for contemplation and the lofty corollary of light, the moss-crowned abbey still, five hundred years after its monks were cast out by a Pope-fearing king, achieves its desired effect. The bones of the majestic masonry come to pervade our own. As we gape, for a while losing awareness of the cold and the nearby meandering couple in matching North Face, we might attribute what stirs within us to God, or the dizzying effect of cavernous spaces upon those of us used to the myopic claustro-phobia of urban density (I remember reading about members of a tribe who had never left their forest being taken to the Grand Canyon and suffering some sort of meltdown as they were unable to process the expansive new perspective). Held by a secular or holy hand, we are somehow pulled out of our-selves by this construction and its design. And it is often when we are removed from ourselves that something *inside* us is transformed. It is not just Rievaulx that acts upon us in this way: we may feel it when visiting far better-maintained city cathedrals. And although nothing there invites us to pay attention within, there is even a dark echo of the same effect as we step into their modern equivalents: vast and sepulchral shopping malls.

Perhaps this is the quieter current of Will at work, and it requires no audio guide. As they extend towards their founders' notion of the Divine, the arches and ribbed ceilings tell us, in truth, less about the Almighty and more about our human capacity to reach out, to persevere towards something unreachable – to *try*, again and again. The ruinous sketch of an abbey that Time has left to us in a silent pocket of the moors' purple-bathed vista outlines the contours of our age-old yearning to reach for the great Other, to connect. Whether or not there is anything up there to be reached, the determined Will to find it is what seems so profoundly human. And the soaring, searching stonework has its musical equivalent in the sacred choral music of the Renaissance era, and later in Wagner. Listen to much of Tallis, or the last few minutes of *Parsifal*'s first act, or the rapturous finale of Elgar's not unrelated *The Dream of Gerontius*, and there in the climbing lines for voices is painted the architecture of Heaven, with its banded golden ranks of seraphim and cherubim. In all these cases there is yearning, and therefore the impetus of Will – not of God's, but of ours.

Perhaps, then, this is in large part what forms our response when we sit in silence, in *in*action, within such places, and let them speak to us. It exists alongside the more evident form of Will which we sense in their construction. Nothing today takes as long to build. We are told that Florence Cathedral, another Gothic masterpiece, took *142 years*, pausing only for the inconvenience of the Black Death. No technology existed to build its intended, now-iconic dome when the first generation of locals picked up their tools and greeted the wagons from Carrara. Standing hushed within it, we are struck by the might of human endeavour and a sheer trust in the future that had all but evaded us in the ninety-minute queue to get in. Today if we conjure a vision of a century and a half ahead of us, there is panic, desolation and guilt. But despite the unimaginable extent of labour needed to realize such places, the history-spanning urge to create and sustain them has persisted, at least until recently, along with their continuing capacity to stir something quiet and primal within us in response. In many of the cathedrals we visit, this private dialogue is masked by a distracting stratum of public life: gift shops and those large board-mounted photo-graphs of disappointingly middle-class congregations captured having a sing-song. But in Rievaulx, sans audio, when all such life has crumbled away and only the green-edged skeleton remains, we see the framework of human longing. Like the basil turning towards the window, it is our Will and nature to reach up and out, again and again. In my Godless vision, though, it is only the act of reaching that sustains us; the photosynthetic analogy falls flat before the last.

These thoughts of the mighty Will evident in such projects and their transcendental effect make daily whinges about our lack of motivation seem misplaced. If at the serene heart of the North York Moors or at the core of a century and a half of Flor-entine toil we can touch the stony resolve of soaring human willpower, and if it is there also in the turning of a basil stem, then perhaps we already have in abundance what it takes to reach our own modest aspirations. I seek frantically to unpack and organize my world to make a home, and meanwhile uncon-sciously, emotionally, the work is being done without the fuss. Perhaps we lean too much upon the rational, executive mind when we need to invigorate ourselves into action. Maybe the Will can show us something about our relentless and surprising undercurrent of power, which flows without conscious effort on our part. Flows, that is, from an emotional base, rather than from our capacity for cognitive control.

The goal-reaching techniques of our age amount to highly rationalized tricks that try to fool our lacklustre emotions into coming onboard, or bypass our feelings altogether. We are very eager to learn how we form good habits. And how we can cheat motivation. Such is the modern obsession with top-down techniques, which have a tendency to read well and inspire effectively on the page, but then come up short in the real world. Let's not treat willpower as a troublesome and evasive beast that needs to be beaten into submission. If Schopenhauer is right, it's bigger than all of us.

Might there be a bottom-up approach instead? One that builds from the bed of our emotions to point this powerful Will in a helpful direction, rather than a hoped-for trickle-down from a set of direct and conscious techniques? Deliberate tactics, whether to form habits or guarantee the seduction of an intended mate, sell themselves as life-hacks, as if they make a strenuous thing easier. But on the briefest examination, they unpack not into a few effective principles but a difficult tangle of procedures for this or that. There is something topsy-turvy in the amount of deliberate work recommended to encourage a single new habit. 'Commit to Thirty Days' demands one site, offering familiar enough advice: 'Make it Daily'. The lingering work ethic of our Protestant forebears still haunts us. The elegant solution, by contrast, is always to change something small to create the largest effect. Also, if the Will's power is unconscious, why do we persist in trying to engage it consciously?

What if we engage with our aims and hopes from this opposite direction? What would we like our emotional resources to achieve if they could be put to use? When we wish to succeed in some plan across time, we need to sacrifice certain short-term pleasures for longer-term benefits. Such is our challenge. Perhaps we must face a fear now because we know the benefits will be worthwhile. We must exercise or choose to study rather than socialize, because it will serve us better in the future. We must in essence learn to shore up our reserves, and persevere in the face of temptation. To rely on sustained conscious effort is to fight a losing battle: it invariably leads to diminishing returns, as we struggle to maintain the fight. It's precisely the worst means of encouraging tenacity.

David DeSteno, of Northeastern University in the US, has written on precisely this topic in his 2018 book *Emotional*

Success, in which he describes a wealth of psychological experiments carried out by his team and others that pinpoint the helpful impact of certain emotions upon our ability to harness our willpower and stick to our plans. It turns out that when we are looking to make better 'intertemporal choices' – that is, to discount pleasures in the here and now in favour of long-term ones – nothing is as effective as being in the grip of a select trio of 'pro-social' feelings. If we can learn to foster these three emotions in our lives, he writes, then we can expect to experience greater levels of self-control when in their grip. The effect, as described by DeSteno, is organic and self-perpetuating – the opposite of the more familiar reliance on our calculated, managerial capacity.

The first of these pro-social emotions is *gratitude*. His finding, played out through repeated experiments with hundreds of volunteers, is that when we are feeling grateful – about anything – we will persevere better with a task, even if it is unrelated to whatever has made us thankful. Thus when subjects of an experiment were made to feel grateful by receiving much-needed help from person X, they were then far more likely to go on to help an unrelated person Y, and for longer. Furthermore, DeSteno describes a series of experiments in which subjects were offered the choice of $100 in a year's time or a smaller amount immediately. On average subjects took only $17 immediately rather than wait for the $100. Gratitude caused them to value that future advantage more. It seems that gratitude 'isn't so much about paying back as about paying forward'. We tend to behave fairly towards others *to benefit our future self.*

DeSteno offers some advice as to how we might increase our levels of gratitude in order to reap these unexpected benefits of perseverance and lending greater weight to future advantage. Keeping a Gratitude Journal may be a very worthy occupation but I fear it is not for me. He also suggests, however, paying more attention to the role of kindness and generosity shown by others in getting us where we are. And while our ultimate aim here – if it is to do better by our future self – might sound oddly self-serving, it is mitigated by the way in which the nature of gratitude triggers an 'upward spiral' of reinforcing benefit. By comparison, we know how hard it is to direct our willpower consciously. We may start well, but we're usually met with those dwindling returns.

The surprising element of DeSteno's trio is *pride*. The most contemptible of the Deadly Sins proves to be another helpful source of tenacity. Deliberately made to feel proud about how well they did in a trivial task, a group of subjects went on to put *40 per cent more time* into solving a difficult problem than others who had not been primed in the same way. It made them more persistent. Similarly, feeling pride increases our ability to resist temptations.

DeSteno's third pro-social emotion is *compassion*. Unlike gratitude and pride, it does not require that a good thing is already in place. Instead, it tends to kickstart a pro-social loop of mutual benefit. Feeling compassion, for the people who populate our lives or simply towards an individual here or there, produces a form of painless, patient self-control. And it may, at least in theory, be a little simpler than gratitude to extend towards ourselves.

We also, after all, populate our own life. We are included in that cast. And we, whenever we reflect, turn out to have only been our past self. As our futures get shorter, there'll come a time when we'll appear to ourselves more like a person who has lived, rather than a person yet to come.

Our relationship with our past can only benefit from a compassionate revision. I have always found my past self something of an embarrassment. Anything I did or said ten years ago seems horrifying. Ten minutes ago could have been far better.

But when I watch old TV shows or performances of mine I am shocked to note that while they are certainly not good, they are often not as profoundly terrible as I'd imagined: my reasoning is that I have always worked with a team of people who have saved me in each instance from myself.

Who would not cringe at their past behaviour? If we are optimistic about the future and pessimistic about the past, then as we have discussed, we are endowed with a certain forward propulsion. Our survival chances are far greater than those of one who can only dwell in fond nostalgia. Hence these self-berating feelings are common; they seem to have an evolutionary value. But a kinder attitude to our bumbling and imperfect younger self is surely of greater benefit than the temptation from which many of us suffer: to see only a catalogue of instances where we have let ourselves down. The compassion generated from adopting a kinder view of our former self might have its own motivational potency and thus serve our *future* self as we move forward through time.

But what it means to extend a softer-hearted attitude towards our younger self will vary for each of us. All sorts of untangling may be required even to consider such a process. So we might prefer another target for a kinder self-view, and that is our *older* self. It is hard to consider such a chimera with benevolence if we can only recoil from our youth. But if I treat my younger self with empathy, it is easier also to pay attention to the needs of what I have not yet become. Now, while I cannot be sure of precisely what those requirements will be, I can make an educated guess. And if I deem them important enough then it makes sense, now, to prepare. There will come a point for each of us, for example, when our main job is to look after ourselves physically. This is neither welcome information nor a natural inclination for those of us who have shirked all forms of exercise since the pre-adolescent humiliation of the football pitch (I scored one goal at primary school, in a moment of uncommon pride and disbelief, and it turned out to be an own goal). But it is worth knowing about, so that I can begin to orient myself towards some forms of exercise before I am completely ruined by touring schedules. Likewise, with my interests veering towards the solitary, I have to apply myself to make sure that I greet the second half of my allotted span with an active social life. We live longer and more happily when we have friends around us. Perhaps it is the stirrings of some unconscious wisdom that make me value them now more than ever.

Considering my older self, my mind drifts back to the craze

for those apps whose arcane algorithms could generate a mocked-up picture of us as old people, and all for the bargain price of placing your private data in the hands of Russian election-hackers. I am surprised to see I still have the software on my phone, and summon it once more. After the inevitable required update, I select the camera mode, and snap a selfie. *Import.* Select *Age.* Select *Old.*

The wrinkled result brings that wave of uncanny horror which quickly fades to a cagey curiosity, rather like spotting a spider in the bath and deciding to calmly observe the shaggy tangle of zigzags rather than flee. Staring at this conjured image of myself, *Do I like this person?* seems the central question. The expression of passionless disinterest is hindering any kindling of affection. So I take another picture, this time smiling warmly as I like to imagine my older counterpart might often do. And it helps enormously: Old Me is now friendly and twinkly. I know, plausible as the fabrication is, that I won't really look like this, any more than Orson Welles grew into Charles Foster Kane or older Brando resembled Vito Corleone. But it will do. The version of me that smiles back is hard to age but has a good white beard and has retained the manly close-cropped hair of my middle age. Behind him is the study in which I currently sit, which reinforces the odd feeling that I shall grow old and die in or near this house, and that these shelves will clutter with old man's things. As I spot a photo of my mother in the background, I note the odd sensation that my mother will not meet this man, that he will be parentless, that he will be more susceptible to the kinds of back problems that I have already encountered when on tour. But nonetheless it does me good to look into the kind eyes of this made-up figure.

I prefer him to the image I was given the first time I used the app a few years ago. I had scrolled around and found a photograph of myself sitting outside a café in Siena, clean-shaven and wearing a summer hat. Nice. Eager to join in with the fun of the new vogue, I imported, swiped, pressed, paused and ... *bingo!* Vinegary Old Poof. Not what I had hoped the impersonal calculations of FaceApp's algorithms would return. But today, this becardiganed, congenial old man has retained a certain sparkle. It is easier to focus a more affectionate attitude upon this furrowed and beaming phantom. No one will know him as well as me, no one else will see as clearly through his pretensions and beyond his grumbling. I can forgive him his enfeebled body, and know that it's as alien and disappointing to him as the thought of it is to me now. His hearing will be bad because mine, weakened by the whumps of pyrotechnics that brought to a nightly close the touring spectacles of my early thirties, already turns most conversations with friendly waitresses into grimacing guessing games. He will have the honour of spending time with my friends and partner – these people I will have spent a large chunk of a lifetime knowing, and come to know myself through. Picturing them in their later years fills me with love. As I conjure the improbably cosy scene of us sitting round the fire in this house, laughing in our cardies (perhaps I never get the insulation sorted), I zoom in on their familiar faces and adore them even more for having lived out a good stretch of life. I hold on to this feeling as I pan across to myself, an animated, whisky-sipping version of the FaceApp extrapolation, and try to imbue him with something like the same fondness.

He may never make it, which makes the thought of his existence even more appealing. Or he may of course, at this very moment, be remembering me too, as he happens upon these words in his personal copy of this book, with its yellow-fringed pages and cover design looking *very* early 2020s. If he's made it that far, I hope he finds it easy to consider me with something of the compassion I am searching for now.

I feel my relationship with the needs of the future soften a little. Perhaps my willpower is not simply some aberrant, lazy creature that is typified by its *un*willingness to show up when most needed. Maybe I already have all the resolve I require. And I think of how it feels when my will is thwarted. It gives me a clue as to its vigorous nature. The days when I have something to be getting on with – typically, at the moment, to write. The misery that arrives when my expectation of doing just that is continually obstructed by the demands of others. What a pig I become. There is this palpable desire for the world of people to dissolve and leave me to get on with what I enjoy. I recognize my irritability as a form of panic as my will is blocked at every turn.

An effective means of avoiding these moods, I have discovered, is to employ the Stoic move of lowering expectations about how the day will progress. I no longer wake up with a vision for myself of happily working all morning and afternoon on personal projects; instead I picture the day unravelling first with tasks and duties, after which my time for treats will find its appropriate place. Without such a stratagem, which sounds obvious in the description but is reluctant to appear so in the bleary mess of a morning, the frantic consternation I experience betrays the single-mindedness of my will.

If the motivational resources I need are strong and already present in abundance, then I may just need to align myself better with them. The cultivation of gratitude, compassion and an appropriate measure of pride may be an effective means of doing that. From a bedrock of these emotions (rather than deliberate executive action), softened by a lowering of expectations (rather than an aggressive elevating of them) and an acknowledgement of the role of others in any success I achieve (rather than fostering an assertive self-belief), there may be an organic route to staying the course where I need to, and to the greatest benefit.

Rievaulx's soaring arches manifest the will-to-connect, shaped in stone and air. The Cistercians were not always the picture of compassion: unusually for monks, they led the violent Albigensian crusade against the heretics of southern France (a unique event in the bloodied catalogue of medieval history, in that the murdered apostates were fellow Christians). But the appetite to find ourselves in another, which has found its way skywards through space and light and centuries of toil, seems not too far from the persevering Will that finds a clear path through such emotions as gratitude and compassion.

At the heart of all of this is a reaching into love. 'Love is wise;

hatred is foolish,' Bertrand Russell famously intoned when asked what advice he might offer to future generations stumbling across his 1959 interview for the BBC. He continued:

> In this world, which is getting more and more closely inter-connected, we have to learn to tolerate each other; we have to learn to put up with the fact that some people say things that we don't like. We can only live together in that way – and if we are to live together and not die together we must learn a kind of charity and a kind of tolerance, which is absolutely vital to the continuation of human life on this planet.

Writ large, the current of our will-to-connect flows verti-cally in search of God, but the same urge also seeks to move quietly and horizontally between us, day after day, where we have the advantage of sometimes being answered. Then, in a third form it can carry us inter-dimensionally forward and backwards through time, to connect with ourselves. And when we do, how uniquely equipped we are to serve the needs of someone desperate to be understood.

HOW TO APPEAR

A few years ago in the UK I took to live television to predict
the National Lottery. At a small studio in Hammersmith I
arranged six ping-pong balls on a stand, each bearing a number selected by members of the public with whom I had been
working in secret. The numbers, for now turned away from
the camera, would serve as the prediction for that night's draw.
Aside from the row of balls, viewers also saw a TV screen set
up to show the live feed from the BBC as it simultaneously
announced the winning numbers on the other channel. Come
the hour, we watched the BBC draw the numbers. A moment
later I turned around the ping-pong balls, which had remained
in shot, to display a perfect match. Bow down before me.

A magic trick, of course. Now, interestingly for our pur-
poses, the ping-pong balls were turned around just *after* the
balls were drawn live. Some viewers suspected a level of camera trickery unfeasible in 2009 on live TV with a handheld

camera. Others raised the question of special ping-pong balls and a carefully positioned laser to print the numbers. 'Any sufficiently advanced technology is indistinguishable from magic,' wrote Arthur C. Clarke in 1962. There is a reverse thread in that line which holds true: when a (probably simple) magic method has proved fooling, people commonly turn to lavish notions of technology to furnish themselves with a working answer. Which is part of the fun.

When we began working through the problems posed by the illusion, we were stumped by one issue: whether we could show the prediction *before* the lottery was revealed. Conceptually, that is what everyone wants, of course. In matters of the mystery arts, to reveal a prediction before the event happens is known as an 'open prediction', and there is always something particularly delicious about the rare times such a thing is possible. If, however, quotidian reality requires you to reveal your prediction just *after* the event, you should offer a good reason. Ours was provided in time by the BBC itself, who had been aware of our plans. Shortly before the broadcast, the venerable institution contacted us to insist upon its right to reveal the lottery numbers before anyone else. Perhaps for the first time in magic history, a magician was *legally required* to show his prediction after the event.

How different the world would be if the future could truly be seen. Or more accurately, from all the many futures which could be easily described, if our own one could be identified. Whether it would help magicians or render them redundant is another puzzle, but unfortunately for all of us hoping to make the best decisions we can, we live life facing the wrong way. 'Most of us live our lives backing into the future, making the choice of each new moment from the data and agenda of the old,' writes James Hollis, a Jungian psychoanalyst and author. With every step forward, we cling possessively to our past. Thus I am rather attached to the story I have stitched together of my unyoked twenties, during which I could paint and read and do whatever I liked. But even this is not my real history, and so I am tethered in my tunnel-vision to an idea of what came before. For all of us, this past remains a secret, obliterated by a wildly misplaced story we have formed in its place. The story is as compelling as the tale of a good magic trick, a series of highlighted moments that blind us to what was happening in the shadows.

Still, as opportunities reach me now, I continue to check in with the inclinations of that younger self to make my decisions: will this new turn threaten my jealously guarded freedom? Choices I make every day rely on the data I feel I have accrued from analogous events or encounters in my past. Meanwhile the truly powerful events of my biography, which reside among those of which I am not conscious, will grasp me the most firmly. We are, as I have already described, living in a meta-phorical alignment with our history.

Of course, then, we repeat ourselves, and arrive at the same situations again and again. To experience relief from this cycle we need to release the magnetic power of much of the past. Try-ing slowly to face the future, we acknowledge that despite our feverish goal-setting, we cannot control what lies ahead. More effectively, as we have discussed, our attention must at some point come to fall gently upon ourselves, and the seeking of an inner congruity which starts within and extends into the rela-tionships of our life. The new orientation is towards growth rather than repetition and regress.

The alternative is a present rooted in the past, and a commitment to a worn-out system. This is a retrospective allegiance that only intensifies when we are tired or panicked. It has given us all we know, including our sense of who we are. Therefore threats to the present order may come disguised as threats to our identity. But that identity is in truth ready to grow and expand through these changes, to rise to each uncertainty. That is why we should not hide from anxieties or frictions: they might be worthwhile and they may signal opportunities for growth. Where we sense them, we can practise leaning in – in towards ambiguity, with the nuance and truth it brings; towards paradoxes which may signal complex truths; towards the disquiet that any opportunity for flourishing must first bring. When our decisions are comfortable, we may be simply replaying our history.

We can unshackle the past from our present by learning to identify the triggers which repeatedly trouble us, or cause problems in our lives. What are the situations that send us hurtling back to face the beasts of our biography? Where do we feel abandoned? Overwhelmed? Some of these attachments may be too raw and painful, and we might require professional help to find breathing space between past and present. But meanwhile, in a hundred more manageable ways, we can look for the snags that reveal our rough edges and cause painful splinters in others. And that project of questioning why our unhappy behaviours persist, what this present reminds us of in the past: this is part of our task, especially in the clearing of midlife.

It is neither a chore to be ticked off nor even a destination to be reached; unserved by shortcuts, it is of course a voyage to be appreciated, and occasionally savoured. We have lights to navigate us: Jung's notion of individuation, and the Stoics' robust image of the self, moving in easier accordance with fate. These provide stories, new myths, to help us find our place. Time, too, plays its part: the undertow will carry us forward in one stage of our life and hold us back in another. Remembering our graph, Time occupies its place upon the y-axis, along with the rest of Fortune whose caprices and dictates lie outside of our control. With our aims constituting the opposing x-axis, we meander along an $x=y$ diagonal as Life and Intention pull us in opposing directions.

In *Happy*, I unfolded the map of Stoicism to offer a means of navigation in an often distressing world. This two-thousand-year-old philosophy, invented by the Greeks and popularized by the Romans, still holds strong, and I am not surprised to see it enjoying a resurgence in our unsettling era. Draw your centre of gravity within. Roll with the punches. Manage your expectations. Relinquish attachment to those things which will be taken from you. Prepare yourself for loss. And find joy in the mastery of a kind of psychological robustness and strength of character they called 'virtue'.

As I described at the end of that book, Stoicism, for me at

least, has its limitations. By the time I had finished writing about it I could sense weaknesses in the system: there was little to be said about compassion, or about community (beyond the value of being a dutiful citizen), and it can be hard to pull off in a relationship. The book you have just read has been an attempt to cover those shaded areas.

In a social world of frustrations, attachments and disappointments, Stoicism remains a very helpful resource. But if there is a tension to be found between the inward mode of the Stoics and the fuller realization of the self through our relationships, it is probably most evident in our romantic entanglements, wherein we both clamour to retain our sense of self and hope to lose it. Given the complex network of sensitivities and varying pathologies that forms within us, we can take comfort in the fact that even a great relationship is routinely taxing for most people.

As I have intimated several times in this book, love is difficult. This may not be saying much, or it may be saying everything, for ten thousand films and love-songs suggest that the only hardship is in *winning* love. Once the prize is claimed it's all happily ever after. As Alain de Botton has written in his wonderful *The Course of Love*, the story is just beginning.

Statements such as *love is difficult* or *love is a prize* don't sound like stories, but they betray their narrative power in the time-lines hidden within those claims. And so they affect us, because whatever story we have in place, we will look for where we stand within it. If love is *supposed* to fall into place like a prize once we win it, if this person is *supposed* to be right for us because we love each other, then we may feel deeply confused and lost when things go wrong. We need a better story, a better idea that can support us when Fortune has the upper hand and for a while we feel the weight of life.

Therefore, let's accept that love is hard. It is not a prize, it is *work*. Like any work it is occasionally a slog, sometimes a chore. We may well love deeply while simultaneously wanting to be left alone. But this is not a fault, because work can also give us a profound sense of meaning and accomplishment. Work can bring us out of ourselves and show us at our best. So let us imagine love as meaningful work, not a shortcut to happiness. Whenever we are trying to achieve something great, we need time to assemble ourselves, to plan and assess, so that we can bring the best of our natures to the project. If we think it's supposed to be easy, we may just throw ourselves into it without care. This may be forgivable in youth, but as we grow we will come to know the importance of privately gathering our strength. 'When you give someone flowers, you arrange them beforehand, don't you?' asks Rilke in his letters. Let's make sure, then, that we arrange ourselves as and when we need to. The distance we need to do that is evident, already there between us, although we may sometimes need to gently claim it.

Without a sense of love as a difficult task, worthy of conscious effort, we have no helpful story when conflict builds upon conflict. We are making the Nouning mistake that we've discussed: feeling scared, we try to organize and calcify, to reduce Love to a static Thing, and the Relationship to something solid. It is not; it never will be: relationships amount to the structure of our lives, and life is all transformation and surprise. Rilke again:

People are so terribly far apart from each other, and people in love are often at the furthest distance. They throw all that is their own to the other person who fails to catch it, and it ends upon a pile somewhere between them and finally keeps them from seeing and approaching each other.

What an accurate image of the challenge of love.

Wonder, like love, comes from leaning into the otherness of

things. An appreciation of mystery that is neither an intellectual cowardice nor an embracing of cheap New Age wonders is surely a key to allowing other worlds to turn, and other human lives space to live and breathe. Stoicism, with its talk of fortification and encouragement of hyper-vigilance, has little to say about otherness. In fact, it can suggest something of a closed shop. There are times to pull down the shutters, but importantly, times to welcome in customers too. Clearly a shop needs other people to survive.

For me, at least, the danger of the Stoic project to minimize disturbance is that such a quest, in flawed people such as myself, can cause atrophy. I am good at remaining calm, and value that enormously. But in my case that brings with it a tendency to avoid healthy challenges, and to loathe confrontations which are sometimes necessary. This is not what the Stoics had in mind, of course.

I prefer to take the strengths of Stoic detachment, and those of the connection-urge we have discussed, and see how they might be synthesized, in that Aristotelian manner I described towards the start of this book. Perhaps by doing so they might combine to form a higher, brighter light to guide us. Martha Nussbaum, who appeared at the start of this book when we were discussing how anger might become useful by undergoing a transition, has given us a helpful synthesis. She recommends that we replace the Stoic notion of a rock standing strong against the lashing waves with the image of a *porous* rock that allows the water to move through it. That helps release the tension, doesn't it?

Another answer: we can move towards a more richly integrated self, of which Jung's vision is helpful. But why might this be important? What is our final imperative as we come to the close of this book? I think the answer is this: *that we remember to appear in our lives.*

The close-up view of our lives does not allow us the perspective we need for the big picture. As with any mosaic, we need to first step back. Most people, wrote Schopenhauer, 'discover when they look back on their life that they have been living the whole time ad interim, and are surprised to see that which they let go by so unregarded and unenjoyed was precisely their life, was precisely that in expectation of which they lived'.

The things to which we pay scant attention might turn out to be the things we are living for. We've seen that midlife is usually when we start to look back, or begin to sense a queasy future nostalgia for the present. Those in-between moments of now, which we forget to enjoy; the shared nothingness of lukewarm daily whiles: these have been piecing together all along to form our lives. Who knew! We thought our life was going to be shaped by the dramatic fulfilment of our plans. For this reason we might one day look back on our allotted time and the hounding we suffered from a thousand external pressures and ask whether we actually, at any point, truly appeared as ourselves.

What might it mean to appear as ourselves in our lives? What would that look like? It's not about shyness and confidence. I think of performers, because so often I'm struck by how the dynamics of a stage show tell me something about life, as we imagined with that card trick. My mind goes to the image of a bad magician, extricating rabbits from outmoded headgear and mutilating his prancing subordinates; gesticulating to overripe music and prattling vapid patter. He might dazzle and even entertain but entirely fail to present himself. We would be left with no sense at all of who he is, and were he to be swapped out with another performer it would make no difference to the act. Could we, in the same way, have been just as easily exchanged for someone else in our own lives? Were we living our life or just following a track, with script, choreography and music stubbornly fixed in place for us?

Usually when we omit to appear in our lives it is because we have been keeping quiet. But absence can take many forms: it is not uncommon to try to dazzle the world while still being a stranger to our own authenticity. Magnificent surfaces deflect attention and give us plenty to hide behind. So appearing in life is not a matter of how we impress upon others, though this may be a forgivable preoccupation of the first half of life. Once we note our middling malaise and stand in need of a new orientation, the fresh invitation is to make sure we appear firmly in our *own* lives, not that of the world. And that is the direction we are heading, the journey we can take on board without an eagerness to arrive at a particular destination, for the meaning of the journey is not to be found at its end.

We don't have to, of course. We can settle for a perfectly fine existence in which we are far more passive about our identity, take our cue from the crowd, and ignore the inchoate yearnings and half-formed questions that stir in the dark. Genuinely, we can. We may even be happy. We may never wonder where we were while it was going on. There is no shame in this, and most decent people are content to take that route. If we do choose the more interesting track, we will frequently lose our way and find ourselves meandering on the well-trodden path, in good company, so we should treat it with respect.

If we do pursue the one route which, it transpires, we must ultimately follow alone, then we may even come to contribute something worthwhile to the world. This is not a prize of ordinary happiness, but that's fine: we're lucky to have had gruff old Beethoven, or the antagonistic, tireless, compassionate figure of J. S. Bach. Hopefully we will experience something of the depth in life that comes from finding ways to maintain an inner congruity, and one which in turn can serve others. We might even know the glimpses of clarity offered by the gentle untangling of threads. Threads that run inwards through our secret, damaged history and outwards into a world of suffering companions.

ACKNOWLEDGEMENTS

Thank you Susanna Wadeson, my editor, for your good will and inhuman patience. Sorry I dragged this out. To Dan Balado for your fresh eyes and brilliant thoughts. To LB for giving me weekends to write, bringing me snacks, and for having to do what is a lot for one person, twenty-four/seven. And to Doodle for belting it across a field when I pretended to collapse and betraying the fact she loves me after all.

SOURCES

(IN ORDER OF APPEARANCE IN THE BOOK)

Greg Lukianoff and Jonathan Haidt, *The Coddling of the American Mind* (2018)

Laurence Scott, *Picnic Comma Lightning* (2018)

Jonathan Haidt, *The Righteous Mind* (2012)

John Bargh, *Before You Know It: The Unconscious Reasons We Do What We Do* (2017)

Martin Lindstrom, *Buyology: Truth and Lies About What We Buy* (2008)

Russell Blackford, *The Tyranny of Opinion* (2019)

Richard Holloway, *Stories We Tell Ourselves* (2020)

Arthur Schopenhauer, *Counsels and Maxims* (1851)

Harry Clor, *On Moderation: Defending an Ancient Virtue in a Modern World* (2020)

Will Storr, *The Science of Storytelling* (2019)

The Social Dilemma (Netflix documentary, 2020)

Michael Moore (writer and director), *Fahrenheit 9/11* (2004)

Martha Nussbaum, *The Fragility of Goodness* (2001)

Clive Thompson, 'Coders' Primal Urge to Kill
  Inefficiency – Everywhere' (*WIRED*, 2019)

Judy Estrin, 'Authoritarian Technology: Attention!'
  (*Medium*, 2018)

Tristan Harris, 'Our Brains Are No Match for Our
  Technology' (*New York Times*, 2019)

Edward O. Wilson, *Debate at the Harvard Museum of
  Natural History, Cambridge, Mass.*, 9 September 2009

Robert Nozick, *Anarchy, State and Utopia* (1974)

Edmund Burke, *A Philosophical Enquiry into the
  Origin of our Ideas of the Sublime and
  Beautiful* (1779)

Philip Shaw, *The Sublime* (2006)

Don McKellar (writer and director), *Last Night* (1998)

Susan Cain, *Quiet* (2012)

Lani Watson, 'What is a Question' (*The Philosophers' Magazine*, 2018)

Leon Festinger, Henry Riecken and Stanley Schachter, *When Prophecy Fails* (1956)

Paul Harris, *The Art of Astonishment* (1996)

Roland Barthes, *Mythologies* (1957)

Martin Heidegger, *Being and Time* (1927)

Jonathan Rauch, *The Happiness Curve* (2018)

John Kaag, *Hiking With Nietzsche* (2019)

Rainer Maria Rilke, *Letters on Life* (2005)

David DeSteno, *Emotional Success* (2018)

Bertrand Russell (BBC interview, 1959)

James Hollis, *Finding Meaning in the Second Half of Life* (2010)

Alain de Botton, *The Course of Love* (2016)

Acknowledgement is also due to the works of Emmanuel Levinas, C. G. Jung and Friedrich Nietzsche

INDEX